POETRY HANDBOOK

Poetry Handbook

A DICTIONARY OF TERMS

by Babette Deutsch

Third Edition: Revised and Enlarged

FUNK & WAGNALLS, NEW YORK

Third Edition, Revised and Enlarged

Acknowledgments—Illustrative Verse

GRATEFUL THANKS are given herewith to the following authors, publishers, and representatives who have so courteously extended permission to use in this Handbook the lines of verse indicated here.

To ALAN SWALLOW. For lines from "Anacreotic" and "Time and the Garden" in Collected Poems by Yvor Winters; copyright, 1952, by Yvor Winters.

To ALFRED A. KNOPF, INCORPORATED. For lines from "Triad" in Verse by Adelaide Crapsey. For lines from "Judith of Bethulia" in Selected Poems by John Crowe Ransom. For lines from Collected Poems by Wallace Stevens.

To BALLANTINE BOOKS, INC. For lines from "The White Sand" by Edmund Wilson in New Poems, Rolfe Humphries, editor.

To BRANDT & BRANDT. For lines from "when / from a sidewalk" in Poems 1923–1954, published by Harcourt, Brace and Company, Inc. Copyright, 1935, by E. E. Cummings.

To Botteghe Oscure. For lines from "A Villanelle" by Babette Deutsch.

To Mrs. Charlie May Fletcher. For lines from "Irradiations" in Preludes and Symphonies by John Gould Fletcher, reprinted by permission of Mrs. Fletcher.

To CHARLES SCRIBNER'S SONS. For lines from "Eclogue of the Liberal and the Poet" by Allen Tate in Poems 1922–1947.

To DODD, MEAD & COMPANY, INC., and SIDGWICK & JACKSON LTD. For lines from "Choriambics II" in The Collected Poems of Rupert Brooke, copyright, 1915, by Dodd, Mead & Company, Inc.

To DOUBLEDAY & COMPANY, INC., MACMILLAN & CO. LTD., and A. P. WATT & SON. For lines from "The Mary Gloster," "The Last Chantey" in The Seven Seas; "The Law of the Jungle" in The Jungle Book; "The Runes on Weland's Sword" in Puck of Pook's Hill—copyright, 1905,

1906, by Rudyard Kipling, and reprinted by permission of Mrs. George Bambridge.

To E. P. Dutton & Co., Inc. For lines from "Homage to John Skelton" in *Animal, Vegetable, Mineral* by Babette Deutsch, copyright, 1954, by Babette Deutsch.

To Faber and Faber Ltd. For lines from *Autumn Sequel* by Louis Mac-Neice. For lines from *Collected Poems 1909–1935* by T. S. Eliot. For lines from *Collected Shorter Poems 1930–1944* by W. H. Auden.

To Funk & Wagnalls Company. For lines from "Lullaby" in *Poems: A Selection.* Copyright, 1954, by Léonie Adams.

To Harcourt, Brace and Company, Inc. For lines from "The Waste Land," "Sweeney Erect," "Preludes," "Ash Wednesday," *The Rock,* and *Four Quartets* in *The Complete Poems and Plays* by T. S. Eliot. For lines from "Statue" and "Looking Into History" in *Things of This World* by Richard Wilbur.

To Harper & Brothers. For lines from *Bolts of Melody, New Poems of Emily Dickinson,* edited by Mabel Loomis Todd and Millicent Todd Bingham.

To Henry Holt and Company, Inc., Jonathan Cape Limited, and The Society of Authors. For lines from "The Laws of God" in *Collected Poems of A. E. Housman.*

To Henry Holt and Company and Jonathan Cape Limited. For lines from "Masque of Reason," "Build Soil," and "Two Leading Lights" in *Complete Poems of Robert Frost.*

To Houghton Mifflin Company. For lines from "Guns as Keys" in *The Complete Works of Amy Lowell.* For lines from *Conquistador* by Archibald MacLeish.

To Hugh MacDiarmid. For lines from "Somersault" in *Speaking for Scotland,* in *Contemporary Poetry;* reprinted by permission of the author.

To James F. Murray, Jr. For permission to reprint from the works of William Carlos Williams.

To The John Day Company, Inc., and Dennis Dobson. For lines from *Selected Verse* by John Manifold.

To Kenneth Rexroth. For lines from "Prolegomenon to a Theodicy" in *The Art of World Wisdom* by Kenneth Rexroth, published by Golden Goose Press.

To Liveright Publishing Corporation, For lines from "At Melville's Tomb" and "The Bridge" in *The Collected Poems of Hart Crane,* copyright, 1933, by Liveright, Inc.

To The Macmillan Company and Faber and Faber Ltd. For lines from "The Jerboa" in *Collected Poems* by Marianne Moore.

To The Macmillan Company. For lines from "Eros Turannos" in *Collected Poems* by E. A. Robinson.

To The Macmillan Company, Macmillan & Co. Ltd., and The Trustees of the Estate of Thomas Hardy. For lines from "The Robin," "Night in the Old Home," "How Great My Grief," "Valenciennes" in *Collected Poems of Thomas Hardy.*

To The Macmillan Company, Macmillan & Co. Ltd., and A. P. Watt & Son. For lines from "The Seven Sages," "Among School Children," and "Under Ben Bulben" in *Collected Poems by W. B. Yeats*.

To Merrill Moore. For lines from "Spotted Hides" in his *The Noise Time Makes*.

To New Directions. For lines from "Paterson I," "Struggle of Wings," "To Waken an Old Lady" in *The Collected Earlier Poems* by William Carlos Williams.

To New Directions and Chatto & Windus Ltd. For lines from "Exposure" in *Poems* by Wilfred Owen. For lines from *Seven Types of Ambiguity* by William Empson.

To New Directions, Faber and Faber Ltd., and Shakespear & Parkyn. For lines from "The Return" and "Night Litany" in *Selected Poems by Ezra Pound*. For lines from "The Bitter Sea" in *Literary Essays by Ezra Pound*.

To New Directions and J. M. Dent & Sons Ltd. For lines from "Ballad of the Long-legged Bait," "Poem on His Birthday," and "Altarwise by Owl-light" in *Collected Poems of Dylan Thomas*.

To Oxford University Press (London). For lines from "Spelt from Sibyl's Leaves," "Inversnaid," "Moonrise," "The Windhover," "The Wreck of the Deutschland," "Sonnet No. 65," and "Pied Beauty" in *Poems* (3rd edition) by Gerard Manley Hopkins.

To Norman Holmes Pearson. For lines from "The Tribute" in *Collected Poems by H. D.* [Hilda Doolittle]. Reprinted by permission of Norman Holmes Pearson and the author, and Liveright Publishing Corporation.

To Random House, Inc. For lines from *The Shield of Achilles* by W. H. Auden, copyright, 1951, 1952, 1953, 1954, 1955, by W. H. Auden; *Collected Poetry* by W. H. Auden, copyright, 1945, by W. H. Auden. For lines from "Eclogue from Iceland" in *Letters from Iceland* by Louis MacNeice (and W. H. Auden), copyright, 1937, by Wystan Hugh Auden. For lines from *Essay on Rime* by Karl Jay Shapiro, copyright, 1945, by Karl Shapiro.

To Routledge & Kegan Paul Ltd. For lines from "Monologue d'outre Tombe" [anonymous] in *Love in Idleness*.

To Southern Methodist University Press. For lines from *Texas Folk Songs* by William A. Owens.

To Vanguard Press, Inc. For lines from "Hornpipe" in the *Collected Poems of Edith Sitwell*, copyright, 1954, and reprinted by permission of the author.

To The Viking Press, Inc. For lines from "Rondeau Redoublé" in *Enough Rope* by Dorothy Parker.

Further Acknowledgments for Second Edition

To City Lights Books. For lines from "Howl" by Allen Ginsberg; copyright, 1956, by Allen Ginsberg.

To ALFRED A. KNOPF, INCORPORATED. For lines from "Chocorua to its Neighbor" by Wallace Stevens, in *The Collected Poems of Wallace Stevens;* copyright, 1943, 1947, 1954, by Wallace Stevens.

To NEW DIRECTIONS. For lines from *The Pisan Cantos* by Ezra Pound; copyright, 1948, by Ezra Pound.

To HOLT, RINEHART AND WINSTON, INC. For lines from "The Lesson for Today" in *Complete Poems of Robert Frost.* Copyright, 1930, 1939, 1943, 1947, 1949, by Henry Holt and Company, Inc.; copyright, 1936, 1942, 1945, 1948 by Robert Frost.

To CHARLES SCRIBNER'S SONS. For lines from "For a Wordfarer" from *Green Armor on Green Ground,* by Rolfe Humphries; copyright, 156, by Rolfe Humphries.

Further Acknowledgments for Third Edition

To Mr. Harold Owen, CHATTO & WINDUS, LTD., and NEW DIRECTIONS. For the first four lines of Wilfred Owen's "Strange Meeting" from *The Collected Poems of Wilfred Owen,* edited with an Introduction and Notes by C. Day Lewis. Copyright, 1963, by Chatto & Windus, Ltd.

To RANDOM HOUSE, INC. For lines from "New Year Letter" by W. H. Auden, from *The Collected Poetry of W. H. Auden;* copyright, 1945, by W. H. Auden; also for lines from "For Friends Only", from "Elegy for J.F.K.", and from "The Cave of Nakedness", by W. H. Auden, from *About The House;* copyright, 1965, 1964, 1963, 1962, 1959, by W. H. Auden.

To THE UNIVERSITY OF NEBRASKA PRESS for "Charm for Bewitched Land" from *Poems from the Old English,* translated by Burton Raffel; copyright 1960, 1964, by The University of Nebraska Press.

Acknowledgments

FOR ATTENTIVE READING of the manuscript of this book, in whole or in part, and for advice, not always followed, I am deeply indebted to a few critical friends, and especially to William A. Owens, to my husband, Avrahm Yarmolinsky, and to a writer who prefers not to be named. Thanks are also due Leroy C. Breunig and Meyer Schapiro for suggestions with regard to certain entries; to Kenneth Yasuda, of The Asia Foundation, Tokyo, for his kind explanation of the shades of meaning in the two Japanese poems of which I made English versions; to Herbert Cahoon, Curator of Autograph Manuscripts, The Pierpont Morgan Library, for his helpfulness in selecting the holograph of Keats's sonnet with the poet's corrections, a reproduction of which serves as the frontispiece. I am also grateful to the many poets, publishers, and other holders of copyright who granted permission to quote illustrative passages, and to whom specific acknowledgments are made on another page.

For suggestions that helped me in preparing the second edition of the book I owe thanks again to my husband and to Leroy Breunig, as well as to W. H. Auden, Rolfe Humphries, Edmund Keeley, and members of the staff of Funk & Wagnalls Company.

I am indebted to John Myhill for critical comment that led to some changes in the third printing of the second edition.

For further observations noted in preparing the third edition I have to thank Allen Tate and Mark Van Doren.

B.D.

By Way of Preface

LIKE DICTIONARIES, poems are made of words. Yet the gulf between the lexicographer's and the poet's way with them seems unbridgeable. The maker of a dictionary assembles a vocabulary that will answer the needs of those apt to consult it. In bringing his words together, the poet is more likely to exact requirements of the reader than to meet his demands. The lexicographer takes into account the history of a word, its roots and relationships, its current spelling and pronunciation, along with its accepted meaning. Conscious of these matters, the versemaker concerns himself with others equally or more closely relevant to the business he has in hand. How complex the stuff of poetry is, linguists, lawyers, and logicians attest, but only one engaged in the craft of verse fully recognizes. The slang phrase: to make with words, literally and figuratively describes his job. Like every other, it has its occupational hazards. Chief among them is the paradox that, on becoming part of a poem, a word exceeds its definition, yet an intrinsic element of poetry is accuracy.

Words are more obviously substantial for the poet than they are even for the phonetician. They have reverberations. They have shapes and shades. They command the meanings that belong to the ordered sounds of one art and to the ordered contours and colors of another. Listening to a word, the lyricist is awake to the fact that it is made up of the letters forming his musical scale, of the syllables composing his chords. So David Jones, appropriately using Welsh and Latin, German and

Cockney, as well as the Queen's English, in his too little known poem, "Anathemata", prints his notes along with the text, "because they so often concern the *sounds* of the words used in the text, and are thus immediately relevant to its *form.* . . ." And, of course, besides the character of his vocables, the songsmith considers the changes that they undergo in different metrical settings. One does not need to know the accompanying music, which shifts from 4/4 to 6/4 time, to hear Ariel's word for his life in freedom change in the twinkling of an eye from the rhythm of gentle pleasure to that of a blithe vivacity:

> On the bat's back I do fly
> After summer merrily.
> Merrily, merrily, shall I live now
> Under the blossom that hangs on the bough.

Aural values play a lively part in the verse of practitioners as diverse as Thomas Campion and Vachel Lindsay, Rudyard Kipling, Walter de la Mare, and Robert Lowell.

The spelling of a word has a significance for the poet that it cannot have for the lexicographer. The former does not write "grey" rather than "gray" because he prefers British to American usage, but because if every vowel has a different hue, as Rimbaud's sonnet reminds us, so does every letter. Indeed, the alphabet approximates not only a musical scale but a gamut of colors. Keats, writing "Of grey cathedrals, buttress'd walls, rent towers", evokes for the responsive eye a darker, colder shade than that of the sea "On the sands of Paumanok's shore gray and rustling", in Whitman's lament. "Splendour" seems to glow with a richer light than the same word deprived of the penultimate letter. Like other subtleties, these have their absurd aspect. There is the story of the pedants who read marvelous meanings into Hart Crane's careless spelling when he wrote of Columbus's logbook consigned to the deep and "floating in a casque" instead of in a "cask". Nevertheless, everything about the look of a word, from the orthography to the size and style of the letters and the arrangement of syllables and phrases on the page in their marginal frame, presents a visual image that is part of the poem. This image, related to but of course distinct from the pictures that the lines summon up, has been a prominent feature in the work of George Herbert, E. E. Cummings, those close contemporaries: Lewis Carroll and Stéphane Mallarmé, as also, more recently, practitioners who favor concrete poetry, such as Ian Hamilton Finlay and Edwin Morgan.

The relationship of poetry to music is an old if not fully understood story. Its kinship with painting was recognized nearly two thousand years ago by the exurbanite lyricist Horace. "*Ut pictura, poesis,*" said he: As the picture, so is the poem. In more ways than the Roman craftsman noticed, the art of verse resembles that of the painter. It is not simply that some works should be looked at closely and others from a distance, some in shadow and others in brilliant light, that some please merely at first showing and others renew their enchantment. Poems, like canvases, present scenes and persons, landscapes, seascapes, and interiors, creatures, figures, faces. And, like paintings of a kind that Horace lived too early to see and never imagined, poems present abstractions.

Words owe their glory, their ugly bristliness, to the fact that they inhabit more than one world. Physical things, formed by the breath, uttered by the mouth, heard by the ear, set down by the fingers, seen by the eye, they always represent things other than themselves. They are signs, but unlike other signs, each points in several directions and functions in various ways. The fire of immediate feeling, thought's lightning illumination, are among their properties. Words represent the concrete objects and the animal necessities among which we live and move and uneasily have our being. Words realize the qualities of an experience intimately known that is yet, without them, inapprehensible. Words reify our ideas of truth, of love, of justice, of life's actual mystery and death's mysterious actuality.

> Death or life or life or death
> Death is life and life is death
> I gotta use words when I talk to you

Sweeney tells Doris in Eliot's fragmentary *Agon*. Not for Sweeney, but for his creator and for every poet, their ambiguous nature contributes paradoxically to their precision, as a mediator's responsibility to each of the conflicting parties is necessary to a satisfactory resolution of a controversy. Words mediate between our ignorance and the sensible universe. They are the cry of our hunger for reality and our means of signifying the strange table spread for us, with its offerings from the sea, where the plankton and the whales and the sharks are swimming, from the deserts with their sphinxes and cities, from the gardens we plant and those we imagine. And when the old enigma in the blankness beyond the space ships and the undiscovered galaxies, or the familiar face in the mirror, stares us out of countenance, we manage to deal with it if we have words.

The finest poet is not necessarily the one with the largest vocabulary. James Joyce, a man who knew nearly a dozen languages and had some acquaintance with about seven times as many, used 29,499 words in *Ulysses* alone. The vocabulary of *Finnegans Wake* has not been estimated but is without question vastly more extensive. Shakespeare, who had little Latin and less Greek and apparently the merest smattering of French and Italian, used a vocabulary of about 20,000 words in his works, that is 6,000 less than the average Swedish peasant in our own time. It would be rash to conclude that this was therefore a lesser mind than the peasant's or that he was a lesser poet than Joyce. With words, as with cattle, uranium deposits, and other kinds of wealth, it is not the extent but the proper control of them that counts. To secure that control the poet must go through an apprenticeship, and he is lucky or wise, which may be the same thing, if he has the right sets of masters and of tools. The present work grew out of the felt need for such a tool: a dictionary of the terms used in discussing verse techniques and some of the larger aspects of poetry, together with examples of poetic practice. Questions about these matters keep arising for readers of verse and for those familiar with the other arts and sciences who would like to know something of this one, as well as for students of literature and for professional poets. The pages that follow supply answers.

This is a book that I wish had been written by one of my betters and available not when I started to write—for I managed a stanza before I could manage a stylus—but when I began to study the craft of verse. Revised editions of such a book should have come out as the understanding of the subject advanced. Nor is it one subject, since a poet should know something about everything that belongs to poetry (and nothing, however abstract, foul, or vulgar, is wholly alien to it) and should know everything there is to know about one thing: verse. Here he depends to some degree on the lexicographer, though he may not surrender to him.

It was observed by the author of the most famous Dictionary in the English language that "Every other authour may aspire to praise; the lexicographer can only hope to escape reproach, and even this negative recompense has been yet granted to very few." While the present volume is a handbook rather than a dictionary, its author is inclined to echo Dr. Johnson, and to add his further comment: ". . . I cannot hope to satisfy those, who are perhaps not inclined to be pleased, since I have not been always able to satisfy myself." Throughout, the effort has been to make the explanations clear and succinct, and to offer suitable illustrative material. Nevertheless, a *mea culpa* must be offered for sins of omission and commission. They are as inevitable in a work of this kind done by one person as they were in the production of the formidable Doctor, especially since the present writer is no such colossus of learning and, though giving definitions that relate to a single field, has had to deal with the accumulated discoveries of many later and more rigorous scholars abroad and at home. In a sense this task was not performed alone, for I looked out diverse authorities on small matters as well as large. Sometimes their analyses seemed too academic or abstruse for a manual of this kind. Sometimes I disagree with their opinions. In any event, for their contributions to my understandings I am deeply grateful.

For the compiler of such a work as this, decisions rear, like a twenty-handed Scylla, a twenty-armed Charybdis, at every turn. Confronting them, I tried to steer a middle course between the pedantic and the popular, to compose a work that would be useful to the general reader without offending the intelligence of the more acute members of the writers' tribe.

The vocabulary of poetics is large. It includes terms relating to the prosody of the ancients and to verse written in Chinese, Japanese, Malayan, Provençal, French, German, Italian, Welsh, as well as in our own tongue. The terms explained here are those meaningful for writers and readers of verse in the English language. There is no definition of the penthemimeral and the hephthemimeral cesura. Such words as crasis, Hipponactean, synizesis, are among those that can be found elsewhere by students concerned with the particulars of Greek and Latin versification. Foreign terms not in general use—*rime suffisante*, for example—are also not given, though *rime riche* is included be-

cause it occurs with some frequency in discussions of English
verse.

A great variety of words describe the different kinds of near
rhyme. These, inclusive of the hippogryphs among them, are
defined under RHYME, in order to distinguish technical terms
that are often misleading yet sometimes valuable. Terms coined
by poets and prosodists that have failed to gain currency have,
however, generally been excluded. Certain words that Gerard
Manley Hopkins used in trying to explain sprung rhythm are
referred to under that definition. When his own-wayish terminology is significant only for students of his work, it is by-passed
on the assumption that they will consult his writings on the
subject. Recent examination of prosodic questions by both
prosodists and linguists has enriched our awareness of technical
procedures. As always, new knowledge means a new vocabulary.
Some respectable old terms begin to look merely old hat. Since
they continue to appear in poetics, however, they require consideration. It is too early to know whether certain fashionable
terms will become a permanent tool of the prosodists, and therefore, not without reluctance, they have been left out.

Self-explanatory references to matters concerning the history
of verse occur in appropriate passages. As a rule, however, terms
that relate to literary history, such as *fin de siècle*, the Celtic revival, surrealism, have been left to the literary historians. There
is little here on subjects treated in ancient works on versification and now of only historical interest, such as "riding rhyme",
a phrase that puzzled Thomas Gray about two centuries ago.

Where a word has several meanings, for the most part only
those that relate to verse are considered. With a few exceptions,
grammatical and rhetorical terms that apply equally to prose
are excluded. This holds, too, for the terminology of phonetics
and of other departments of linguistics proper. Though this is
one of the poet's chief concerns, he is not apt to require the

technical vocabulary, nor even to use the phonetician's approach as consciously as John Thelwall, who composed a "Song Without a Sibilant" that begins:

> No, not the eye of tender blue,
>   Though, Mary, 'twere the tint of thine,
> Or breathing lip of glowing hue
>   Might bid the opening bud repine,
>   Had long enthrall'd my mind.

There are some arbitrary omissions, such as "daemon", which governs any possessed genius, though the Muse is included, because, often in the guise of Robert Graves' White Goddess, she is peculiarly associated with poetry. Myth, which does not inform this art exclusively, is referred to under MYTHOPOESIS.

As far as possible, the definitions are illustrated with lines of verse, one or more stanzas, and, on occasion, entire poems. Appended to the text is a list of the poets cited, with their dates, and the pages on which their names occur. It ranges from the ancients to members of today's avant-garde, and includes verse-makers hailing from the Far East, from "down under", from Europe, as well as from home. Not all the memorable poets are represented, although some lesser ones are here, since the effort was not to choose important names but to find passages that would illustrate the point in question. The extent of the quoted matter is curtailed partly by the excessive demands of one poet and partly by limitations of space. Where attribution is lacking, the quoted passage or poem is by the author of this book.

A few forms not commonly used have been indicated but not exemplified under the definition of stanza. The Wordsworthian sonnet, as a variant not warranting separate reference, is considered under SONNET. The choice of quotations was a business as full of bloody thorns and brambles, rich colors, fine fragrances, as gathering bouquets in an incomparable rose garden that led into meadows and forests tapestried with wild flowers. The problem presented was almost as fascinating as it was difficult.

There were other problems that had no mollifying circumstances. Volumes have been written on such subjects as imagination and symbol, as well as on several of the technical aspects of verse. How reduce the acute, subtle discriminations in these books to a few plain, concise statements? Impossible. Aristotle has it that "the poet should prefer probable impossibilities to improbable possibilities." I would not, if I could, have forgotten the duties and privileges of a poet in making this handbook, and so there are pages in which I attempted an impossibility that seemed to have an air of the probable.

BABETTE DEUTSCH

New York, 17 September 1956

NOTE TO THE SECOND EDITION

In his old age, after assuring a friend that there was nothing wrong with the syntax in one of her poems, Yeats confessed that he had never understood the meaning of the word. Since she too pleaded uncertainty, he made her fetch a dictionary: perhaps they *ought* to know what syntax was. On looking it up myself, I found that, in addition to its usual meanings of orderly arrangement and established grammatical usage, in seventeenth-century England it was also the name of a class in some Roman Catholic schools and colleges; the class above it was called *Poetry*. Syntax can be dispensed with by the genius, but even Yeats asserted that poets cannot dispense with anything that adds to their knowledge of the craft. The interest that contemporary poets, along with the common reader, have shown in this little book has encouraged me to revise and enlarge the original text. The changes have been limited by the wish to add nothing to the price of the book, while trying to increase its usefulness.

B.D.

New York, 8 August 1961

NOTE TO THE THIRD EDITION

When it was demanded of Dr. Johnson to say "what is poetry", he replied, "Why, Sir, it is much easier to say what it is not. We all *know* what light is; but it is not easy to *tell* what it is." This book does not pretend to contain matter that would instruct the venerable Doctor. But it does respect the view of two diverse and notable practitioners that a poem is a machine made of words or a verbal artifact, and therefore among the proper concerns of a poet are the devices and strategies that make such a machine work. The illustrative material, which ranges from an Old English charm to lines by recent comers to the craft, may possibly also illuminate the larger subject of poetry.

The present edition corrects errors that inadvertently crept into earlier ones. Not a little of the original material has been expanded, and new entries, such as alphabet poem, concrete poetry, confessional poetry, projective verse, find a place here. The task of putting together this third edition has been a rewarding one for the author, who dares hope that the finished work will prove so to its readers.

B.D.

New York, 7 January 1969

POETRY HANDBOOK

A Word to the Beginner

THERE ARE MANY terms for the various ways in which the poet makes words work. This *Handbook* includes such as seem of greatest significance for the reader and the student of poetry. Those who have little knowledge of the field may find their way more readily if they first consider entries that apply to the art generally and then turn to some that deal with technical procedures.

Wordsworth once remarked, rather astonishingly, that "the matter always comes out of the manner." He was speaking of style, but the implication is that the form of a work governs its content. This might be debated. What is undeniable is that manner and matter, the theme and the way in which it is expressed, the meaning and the structure, cannot be separated without vital injury to the poem. Nevertheless, since the anatomy of verse is important to an understanding of poetry, we may temporarily anesthetize the poem, as it were, lay it on the table, and examine distinct parts of it. But we know very well that only when these organs or members, which we are studying separately, function together in one body will the poem breathe and move like the living thing it is.

The reader might start his inquiry with the definition of POET. Going on to POETRY, he will find the definition given by the author supplemented by others offered by a number of notable poets, from Spenser to Dylan Thomas. Here, too, the difference between the art of poetry and the craft of verse is noted.

The exploration of technique may commence with RHYTHM, and continue with the more exacting subject of METRE. In connection with this, the reader may wish to study the PROSODIC SYMBOLS and to read the entry on SCANSION. Consideration of the workings of metre may be followed by that of RHYME and then of STANZA. There are a number of other entries that define specific technical terms. The reader may choose to explore the various definitions connected with one large subject before considering the next. Thus RHYTHM would lead him to examine FREE VERSE, SPRUNG RHYTHM, and SKELTONICS, as well as METRE, while STANZA might send him to FRENCH FORMS and other related terms. Under such entries as METRE and RHYME, which discuss at length one feature of the craft, the reader will be apt to come upon unfamiliar terms. Those that are not explained in the passage in which they occur are defined in a separate entry.

Occasionally it may be helpful to interrupt the reading of an extensive entry, such as METRE, by turning to others, like COMPENSATION and ELISION, that bear on the discussion. Just as in making a bonfire or building a bridge, so in making a poem one must bring into close relation things widely separated, and yet seem to have them all in hand at once. Studying the craft of poetry demands something of the same kind of skill and agility. It demands, too, an understanding of matters not obviously connected with questions of technique, as the definition of the art suggests. The student ready to consider those aspects of it may find helpful such entries as IMAGE, CONNOTATION, TEXTURE, IMAGINATION, METAPHOR, and SYMBOL.

The reader will, of course, be guided by his own needs. He may wish to disregard the suggested sequence and simply browse here and there. He may read this *Handbook* as some people like to read any dictionary, intrigued by uncommon terms and by the insights that fresh definitions offer. Running his eye down successive pages, he will pass from ALCAICS and

ALEXANDRINE to AMBIGUITY and AMPHIBRACH, perhaps pausing to look up ALLEGORY under METAPHOR and ALLITERATION under RHYME. Whatever course he prefers, it is hoped that this book will confirm him in the conviction that poetry as an art is intimately bound up with verse as a craft.

B. D.

[A]

abstract poem A term used by Dame Edith Sitwell for verse that depends chiefly upon its auditory values for its meaning. Such poetry is analogous to abstract painting in which the arrangement of colors and shapes is significant though no physical objects are represented. Words are employed with little regard for their usual connotations, but rather for their aural effectiveness in a pattern of full and approximate rhymes and in the manipulation of rhythm. Her own poems in the collection called *Façade* exemplify the type, which may be illustrated by three lines from her lively "Hornpipe" where, we hear, the dumb

> Sky rhinoceros-glum

> Watched the courses of the breakers' rocking-horses and with
> Glaucis
> Lady Venus on the settee of the horsehair sea!

acatalectic See **catalectic**.

acatalexis The use of an acatalectic line.

accent Emphasis on a syllable. Some prosodists distinguish between the terms "stress" and "accent" in order to clarify the different kinds of emphasis. These writers use "stress" when referring to metrical stress and reserve "accent" for the emphasis demanded by the language. Such emphasis is called **etymological, grammatical,** or more simply **word accent.** The emphasis that in normal speech falls on a heavily stressed syllable is the **primary accent (´).** The emphasis that in normal speech falls on a lightly stressed syllable is the **secondary accent** (ˋ). Shelley's line "Ah, sister! Desolation is a delicate thing:" exhibits both primary and secondary accents in the word "dès o lá tion." Usually, as here, a primary accent coincides with the metrical stress. An **even accent** or **level stress** is one which falls with equal emphasis on two syllables in a dissyllabic or polysyllabic word, as in man'kind' and wa'ter-worn' and sometimes occurs when two monosyllabic words are closely associated, such as old' man'. In verse it has the effect of DISTRIBUTED STRESS. See also **recessive accent**.

accentual verse   See **metre**, page 88.

accentual-syllabic verse   See **metre**, page 88.

acephalous line   A headless line. See **catalectic**.

acrostic   A poem in which the initial letters of the lines spell a name or a title. Thus, Ben Jonson prefaces *The Alchemist* with

THE ARGUMENT

T he sickness hot, a master quit, for fear,

H is house in town, and left one servant there.

E ase him corrupted, and gave means to know

A cheater and his punk; who, now brought low,

L eaving their narrow practice, were become

C oz'ners at large; and, only wanting some

H ouse to set up, with him they here contract,

E ach for a share, and all begin to act.

M uch company they draw, and much abuse,

I n casting figures, telling fortunes, news,

S elling of flies, flat bawdry, with the Stone—

T ill it, and they, and all in fume are gone.

See also **alphabet poem.**

aesthetic distance   The effect produced when an experience, removed from other irrelevant, haphazard experiences, is organized and framed by the formal limits of a poem, so that it can be contemplated and more fully understood.

alba   See **troubadour,** page 183.

alcaics   A stanza in the metre invented by the Greek poet Alcaeus, and later used in a slightly altered form by the Roman poet Horace. The original metre was imitated by Tennyson thus:

> Ō mīghty̆-mōuthed īnventŏr ŏf harmŏnĭes,
>
> Ō skīll'd tŏ sīng ŏf Tīme ŏr Ĕtērnĭty̆,
>
>   Gōd-gīftĕd ōrgăn-vōice ŏf Ēnglănd,
>
>   Mīltŏn, ă nāme tŏ resōund fŏr āges; . . .

alexandrine   This twelve-syllable iambic line takes its name from the fact that it is related to that used in the Old French romance on Alexander the Great. The classical French alexandrine differs from ours in having two principal stresses which fall on the sixth and the last syllable and one light stress with no fixed place in each half line. It may be heard as a tetrameter in triple time, as in Racine's famous line:

> C'est Vénus / toute entière / à sa proie / attachée.

Having become the accepted metre for classical tragedy in French, the line developed something of the flexibility of our iambic pentameter. Phonetic experiments with the French alexandrine show that, while the poet is constrained to adhere to the twelve-syllable line, in recitation the number of syllables may range from eight to fourteen, the number and place of the stresses depending on the context. This seems natural to a language having no fixed word accent. The English alexandrine is illustrated in the second line of Pope's couplet:

A needless alexandrine ends the song
That, like / a wound / ed snake, / drags its / slow length / along.

Robert Bridges spoke of "my loose alexandrines" in *The Testament of Beauty*. These are twelve-syllable lines, unstressed and unrhymed. Additional syllables are admitted by the use of elision, as the following excerpt shows:

> Beauty is the highest of all these occult influences,
> the quality of appearances that thru' the sense
> wakeneth spiritual emotion in the mind of man:
> And Art, as it createth new forms of beauty,
> awakeneth new ideas that advance the spirit
> in the life of Reason to the wisdom of God.

allegory   See **metaphor**, page 82.

alliteration   See **rhyme**, page 131.

alphabet poem   One that resembles an ACROSTIC insofar as it is built on the first letters of the lines—here, the 26 letters of the alphabet. Paul West, the inventor, allows himself certain liberties, such as the occasional use of the Greek or Russian alphabet, and the introduction of "ex-" compounds. He has worked out an elaborate scheme of 26 poems, each thirteen lines long, every line comprised of two words, the first poem starting AB and ending YZ, the second starting BC and ending ZA (A following Z throughout), the last starting ZA and ending XY. He does not encourage the complexities of metre and rhyme, although the latter can occur, as witness this example:

Artichokes, Bubbly,
Caviar, Dishes
Epicures Favor,
Gourmets Hail;
Ices, Juicy
Kickshaws, Luxurious
Mousses, Nibblesome
Octopus, Pheasant,
Quiches, Sweets,
Treats Utterly
Vanquish Weightwatchers:
Xenodochy's
Yum-yum!

ambiguity   This occurs when double or multiple meanings attach to words or to situations. All figurative language is somewhat ambiguous. While an ambiguity is never desirable for its own sake, in poetry, as distinct from scientific discourse and much other prose, it may be useful. By competing, several meanings can illuminate more fully the complexities of the experience that the poem offers. William Empson, who has intensively explored seven varieties of ambiguity, defines it as "any verbal nuance, however slight, which gives room for alternative reactions to the same piece of language". The first type arises when "a detail is effective in several ways at once"; the second when "two or more alternative meanings are fully resolved into one"; the third when "two apparently unconnected meanings are given simultaneously"; the fourth when "the alternative meanings combine to make clear a complicated state of mind in the author"; the fifth is "a fortunate confusion, as when the author is discovering his idea in the act of writing . . . or not holding it all in mind at once"; the sixth occurs when "what is said is contradictory or irrelevant and the reader is forced to invent interpretations"; the seventh type is one "of full contradiction, marking a division in the author's mind". A glance at an example of the first type will indicate Empson's procedure. He instances Shakespeare's line, "Bare ruin'd choirs, where late the sweet birds sang" and shows the various ways in which wintry boughs, themselves emblematic of the poet's deprived state, resemble "bare ruin'd choirs". Among the less obvious are "the protestant destruction of monasteries" and the fact that "the cold and Narcissistic charm suggested by choir-boys suits well with Shakespeare's feeling for the object of the sonnets . . .". These and half a dozen other ways of realizing the comparison both complicate and enrich it, which is the function of any form of ambiguity in a poem.

amphibrach   A foot consisting of three syllables, the first short or unstressed, the second long or stressed, the third short or unstressed. See also **metre**.

amphimacer   A classical foot of three syllables, the first long or stressed, the second short or unstressed, the third long or stressed. It thus reverses the order of the AMPHIBRACH, which is more usual in English verse.

amphisbaenic rhyme   See **rhyme**, page 131.

anacreontics   Lyrics praising wine, women, and song, composed in imitation or adaptation of those by the Greek poet Anacreon, and often written in trochaic tetrameter. These lines translated by Stanley are typical:

> Fruitful earth drinks up the rain;
> Trees from earth drink that again;
> The sea drinks the air, the sun
> Drinks the sea, and him the moon.
> Is it reason then, d'ye think,
> I should thirst when all else drink?

Graver lines are sometimes described as anacreontic. The term
is the title of a poem by Yvor Winters which concludes:

>   Come, write good verses, then!
>   That still, from age to age,
>   The eyes of able men
>   May settle on our page.

anacrusis   The admission of one or two unstressed syllables
at the start of a line of verse that do not count as part of the
metre. The last line of this stanza by Blake exemplifies it:

>   Innocence doth like a rose
>   Bloom on every maiden's cheek;
>   Honour twines around her brows,
>   The jewel health adorns her neck.

analyzed rhyme   See **rhyme**, page 131.

anapest   A foot of three syllables, the first two short or unstressed, the last long or stressed. See also **metre**, page 88.

anapestic   See **metre**, page 88.

Anglo-Saxon prosody   Based on the principles of stress and
alliteration, each line is composed of two half lines separated by
a pause. Normally every hemistich has two stressed syllables
making four to the line. The first three stressed syllables in the
line are alliterated. Stress falls on a long syllable or on the first
of two short syllables. Usually stress and alliteration emphasize
meaning. A close approximation to Anglo-Saxon verse is found
in English poems composed during the alliterative revival of the
fourteenth century, among them that about Piers the Plowman
who, dressed as a shepherd,

>   Went wýde   in this woŕld . Wońderes to heŕe.

See also **metre**, page 88; **rhyme**, page 131.

anthology   Literally "gathered flowers", the word has come to mean a collection of admirable pieces of literature, often of poems. A reference to *The Anthology* is to a collection of some 4500 short Greek poems composed approximately between 490 B.C. and A.D. 1000.

anti-poetic, the   See **poetic diction.**

antistrophe   See **ode.**

apocopated rhyme   See **rhyme, page 131.**

approximate rhyme   See **rhyme, page 131.**

argument   The prose sense or statement of a poem, such as Spenser offers as introductions to his eclogues, Milton to the cantos of *Paradise Lost,* and Coleridge in his marginalia to *The Rime of the Ancient Mariner.*

arsis   See **thesis.**

assonance   See **rhyme, page 131.**

aubade   See **troubadour, page 183.**

[B]

backward rhyme   See **rhyme**, page 131.

ballad   A short simple narrative poem, the **folk ballad** was anonymous, composed to be sung, and altered as it was repeated, from generation to generation and in different regions, without being written down. "A wilding from the garden of chivalry" Grierson calls it, since the earliest of these stories in verse were founded on dramatic incidents from the old romances or upon some older legend. The ballad presents a romantic theme, impersonally treated, and is characterized by the simplicity of the language, the repetition of epithets and phrases, the casual handling of rhyme, the liberties allowed by stress prosody. The **ballad stanza** is a ^{4} b ^{3} c ^{4} b ^{3}. In *A Midsummer Night's Dream* Quince suggests that the prologue to the play "be written in eight and six", the numerals referring to the syllables, while Bottom demands that it be "written in eight and eight", another popular measure, used in ballads. The rhymes in a ballad are often approximate. A refrain is not unusual. The folk ballad which flourished in fifteenth-century England and Scotland has lived on into our own time in the southern Appalachians and other secluded areas. A comparison between an early Scottish version of two stanzas from "Edward" and one sung by a Texas woman in 1941 suggests what transformations a ballad may undergo.

> "Your hawk's blude was never sae red,
> Edward, Edward;

Your hawk's blude was never sae red,
   My dear son, I tell thee, O."
"O I hae kill'd my red-roan steed,
   Mither, mither;
O I hae kill'd my red-roan steed,
   That erst was so fair and free, O."

"How come that blood on your shirt sleeve
My son come telling to me?"
"It is the blood of the old gray mare
That pulled the plow for me."

The medieval ballad has its counterpart in our cowboy ballads, in verse narratives about frontiersmen and a few about heroes of the labor movement in the days when its history was full of violence. The folk song of the late twentieth century is less apt to be about a particular character, but not seldom carries political or social overtones. It is the work of known songsmiths, such as Simon and Garfunkel, among others.

The **literary ballad** is a skilled craftsman's imitation of the anonymous popular form. He may try to reproduce or closely approximate the features of the folk ballad, as Keats did in "La Belle Dame Sans Merci". He may use the same form for a poem full of private symbolisn, as Dylan Thomas did in his "Ballad of the Long-Legged Bait", which is open to several interpretations. These are the first and final stanzas:

The bows glided down, and the coast
Blackened with birds took a last look
At his thrashing hair and whale-blue eye;
The trodden town rang its cobbles for luck.

Good-bye, good luck, struck the sun and the moon,
To the fisherman lost on the land.

He stands alone at the door of his home,
With his long-legged heart in his hand.

The poet may develop a different structure, retaining only some elements of the older verse narrative, as Kipling did in his *Barrack Room Ballads* and as R. P. Warren has done in a far more sophisticated poem, "The Ballad of Billie Potts", in which the dramatic narrative is interspersed with the poet's commentary on history and identity in a fashion foreign alike to the folk ballad and the literary ballads of Keats, Coleridge, Kipling, and Thomas. See also **common measure.**

ballade   A poem normally composed of three stanzas and an envoy, the last line of the opening stanza used as a refrain, and the same rhymes, strictly limited in number, recurring throughout. Originally the number of lines in the stanza varied from one ballade to another, and some omitted the envoy. It is now usual for the stanza to consist of eight lines on three rhymes with an envoy half its length. The preferred metre is iambic or anapestic tetrameter, but others are used. There is no deviation from the rhyme scheme. The **envoy** is in the nature of a dedication to a person of importance or to a personification and is also a climactic summary. Another scheme often employed has a ten-line stanza, usually pentameter, rhymed *a b a b b c c d c D*, with the envoy *c c d c D*. This form is exemplified in the first stanza and envoy of Villon's "Ballade of the Hanged" in the version by Swinburne:

Men, brother men, that after us yet live,
        Let not your hearts too hard against us be;
For if some pity of us poor men ye give,
        The sooner God shall take of you pity.
Here are we five or six strung up, you see,
        And here the flesh that all too well we fed
Bit by bit eaten and rotten, rent and shred,

And we the bones grow dust and ash withal;
Let no man laugh at us discomforted,
But pray to God that He forgive us all.

ENVOY

Prince Jesus, that of all art Lord and Head,
Keep us, that Hell be not our bitter bed;
We have nought to do in such a master's hall.
Be ye not therefore of our fellowhead,
But pray to God that He forgives us all.

The eight-line form admits a double refrain, the fourth as well
as the final line being repeated in each octave and in the envoy.
The scheme for the stanza is then *a b a B b c b C* and that for
the envoy *b B c C*. The first stanza and envoy of Henley's
"Ballade of Youth and Age" give a glimpse of the arrangement:

Spring at her height on a morn at prime,
Sails that laugh from a flying squall,
Pomp of harmony, rapture of rhyme—
Youth is the sign of them, one and all.
Winter sunsets and leaves that fall,
An empty flagon, a folded page,
A tumble-down wheel, a tattered ball—
These are a type of the world of Age.

ENVOY

Struggle and turmoil, revel and brawl—
Youth is the sign of them, one and all.
A smouldering hearth and a silent stage—
These are a type of the world of Age.

The **double ballade** is composed of six octaves or ten-line stanzas
on three and four rhymes, respectively, with the refrain but
seldom including an envoy. Alfred Noyes wrote a triple ballade
of nine octaves and an envoy.

The **chant royal** alters the ballade structure, using five stanzas, each of eleven lines, and a five-line envoy, with the customary refrain. The normal rhyme scheme for the stanza is *a b a b c c d d e d E*, that for the envoy *d d e d E*. Originally employed for the development of an allegory which was explained in the envoy, this form is as rare in English verse as it is intricate.

ballad stanza   See **ballad; common measure.**

bard   One whose gifts and long training fitted him to compose and recite the poems with which the ancient Celts honored their heroes. The term has become synonymous with poet, especially when regarded as a singer of heroic exploits. Frost—in lines "To a Thinker"—arguing reasonably against using one's mind too hard, urges the man to "trust my instinct—I'm a bard".

baroque   The Portuguese word from which this term is derived means an irregularly shaped pearl, so that connotations of the bizarre and the opulent seem appropriate. Originally the word described the florid architecture of a period dating roughly from the mid-sixteenth century through part of the eighteenth. It has come to be applied to literature, and particularly to poetry, some scholars delimiting the period of baroque writing more narrowly. Imbrie Buffum describes the style as resting on "a Christian sensibility" and characterized by excess and "a strong will toward" the good. He holds that it exhibits an awareness of both the beauty and the horror of the diverse, dynamic, physical world; an "almost perverse pleasure" in shock, and hope for the eventual triumph of the highest values. Wylie Sypher sees baroque as a "sumptuous, pompous, invigorating, fleshly, authoritarian" style—an exuberant and resonant declaration of "the glories of heaven and earth", with the emphasis on "earth". He finds its significant features include "august equilibrium" as well as "expressive energy" and cites as instances of baroque two of Milton's poems, *Samson*

Agonistes and *Paradise Lost.* Since, in his view, the exercise of
the will is the most authentic expression of baroque power, he
places Satan "at the center of baroque art" when he puts the
question:

> . . . What though the field be lost?
> All is not lost; the unconquerable Will,
> And study of revenge, immortal hate,
> And courage never to submit or yield;
> And what is else not to be overcome?

As Sypher recognizes, the style can lead to absurdities. Dryden
in his youth produced an instance of baroque verse in his elegy
on Lord Hastings, who died of smallpox. An excerpt follows:

> Blisters with pride swell'd, which through flesh did sprout
> Like Rose-buds, stuck i'the Lily'skin about.
> Each little Pimple had a tear in it,
> To wail the fault its rising did commit . . .
> Or were those gems sent to adorn his Skin
> The Cab'net of a richer Soul within?

The usual examples of baroque writing come from the work of
Richard Crashaw, whose sensuous conceits appear in these clos-
ing lines of the "Prayer" that he composed in the form of "An
Ode, which was Prefixed to a little Prayer-book given to a
young Gentlewoman":

> O let the blissful heart hold fast
> Her heav'nly armful, she shall taste
> At once ten thousand paradises;
> > She shall have power
> > To rifle and deflower
> The rich and roseal spring of those rare sweets
> Which with a swelling bosom there she meets

> Boundless and infinite
> Bottomless treasures
> Of pure inebriating pleasures.
> Happy proof! she shall discover
> What joy, what bliss,
> How many Heav'ns at once it is
> To have her *God* become her *Lover*.

The term is also broadly used to describe poems, regardless of their period, that display vehement feeling extravagantly expressed. Modern instances of baroque poetry can be found in the work of Dame Edith Sitwell and of Dylan Thomas.

beat   The term characterizes the work of those of our contemporaries who reject the values of the society into which they were born and who often express their rejection in scatalogical imagery, using the jargon of the jazz world. Their disaffection may issue in an outburst like Allen Ginsberg's "Howl", which opens:

> I saw the best minds of my generation destroyed by
>   madness, starving hysterical naked,
> dragging themselves through the negro streets at
>   dawn looking for an angry fix,
> angleheaded hipsters burning for the ancient heavenly
>   connection to the starry dynamo in the machinery
>   of night, . . .

As these lines suggest, for the writers who accept the epithet, it does not carry the connotation of "beaten" but rather of their search, by the artificial means that Rimbaud recommended, for beatitude. Indeed, one of their anthologies bears that title. Because of their rootlessness, their ribaldry, their explosive attacks on the accepted order, they might be called the goliards of the atomic age, but the term is only partially apt, since they lack the ecclesiastical background, the witty scholarship, the technical skill, and the natural gaiety of their medieval predecessors.

blank verse   Unrhymed verse, such as is found in Charles Lamb's "The Old Familiar Faces", which opens:

> I have had playmates, I have had companions,
> In my days of childhood, in my joyful school-days—
> All, all are gone: the old familiar faces.

Usually, however, the term refers to the verse employed by Milton in *Paradise Lost*. This he described in his preface to the poem as "English Heroic verse, without Rime . . .", proceeding to defend its use. His best defense lay in the poem itself, the opening lines of which follow:

> Of Mans first Disobedience, and the Fruit
> Of that Forbidden Tree, whose mortal tast
> Brought Death into the World, and all our woe,
> With loss of *Eden*, till one greater Man
> Restore us, and regain the blissful Seat,
> Sing Heav'nly Muse, . . .

A recent example comes from Robert Frost's A *Masque of Reason*, in which God says:

> Job, you must understand my provocation.
> The tempter comes to me and I am tempted.
> I'd had about enough of his derision
> Of what I valued most in human nature.

breve   See **mora.**

broken rhyme   See **rhyme**, page 131.

bucolic poetry   See **pastoral.**

burden   See **stanza**, page 169.

Burns stanza   See **stanza**, page 169.

[C]

cadence   Used sometimes as a synonym for RHYTHM or for METRE, the word may more properly be defined as a rhythmical unit, similar to a musical phrase, which, when recurring, gives symmetry to verse where a strict metrical pattern is wanting. Related to the Latin word meaning "to fall", it reminds one of Orsino's plea in *Twelfth Night*: "That strain again, it had a dying fall." The word "dying", which carried sexual connotations to Elizabethan ears, may have been intended as a pun, but in any event it is clear that the lovesick Duke was speaking of a melody in terms that might apply to a poem. Cadence is also used of a work characteristic of a poet or of the movement of a poem. Thus one may refer to "a Miltonic cadence" or to "the cadences of 'Dover Beach' ". See also **free verse**.

calligramme   A term used by Apollinaire to describe poems in which the arrangement of the typography helps to present the theme. A simple instance is his poem, "It Rains", which is printed in wavering vertical lines. This device, which was used by the ancients, is also displayed in George Herbert's wing-shaped "Easter Wings" and in the womb-shaped or chalice-shaped poems of Dylan Thomas's "Vision and Prayer". The French poet manipulated typography more surprisingly than they, but never achieved the extraordinary effects of E. E. Cummings. In his poem about a discarded Christmas tree, the "X" of "X-mas" is isolated so as to suggest at once the mystery

and marvel of the holiday and its inglorious exit. See also
concrete poetry.

canso   This term is sometimes restricted to a Provençal love
song of five, six, or seven stanzas plus an envoy, the lines not
necessarily of equal length, with interlacing masculine and
feminine rhymes. See also **troubadour**, page 183.

canto   One of the major divisions of a long poem, such as
those of the "Inferno", the "Purgatorio", and the "Paradiso",
which together comprise the one hundred cantos of *La Divina
Commedia*. Reference to *The Cantos* is to the otherwise untitled poem by Ezra Pound, which, when completed, was at one
time to have equalled Dante's in the number of its divisions,
but has since been extended.

canzone   See **troubadour**, page 183.

catalectic   A line from which unstressed syllables have been
dropped. Such lines are also called **truncated.** The procedure is
called **catalexis** or **truncation.** When the unstressed syllables
are dropped at the start of a line, it is **headless.** This device can
lend force to a statement, as in the second line of Housman's
couplet:

> And if my ways are not as theirs
> Let them mind their own affairs.

In trochaic verse the final syllable is often dropped, as in the
first two lines of Shelley's stanza:

> Music, when soft voices die,
> Vibrates in the memory—
> Odours, when sweet violets sicken,
> Live within the sense they quicken.

The third and fourth lines have their full complement of syllables and are therefore **acatalectic. A hypercatalectic** line has one

or more syllables in excess of the normal. Such lines are also described as **hypermetrical** or **extrametrical**. These adjectives are applied to syllables that do not count as part of the metre. Milton sometimes allowed an extrametrical syllable in the decasyllabic verse of *Paradise Lost* to enforce the meaning of the words, as here, "Deliberate valour breath'd, firm and unmov'd" See also **substitution.**

catalexis   See **catalectic.**

caudated sonnet   Tailed sonnet. See **sonnet,** page 161.

cento   A patchwork poem, made up of scraps from various sources, such as these lines:

> To shop in crowds the daggled females fly;
> Tired with all these, for restful death I cry,
> Care-charming Sleep, thou easer of all woes,
> Soft as the fleeces of descending snows.
> Now let the night be dark for all of me.
> O, pray for us, the bourgeoisie.

The authors are Swift, Shakespeare, Fletcher, Pope, Frost, and Auden.

cesura   A pause in the reading of a line of verse that does not affect the metrical account of the timing. It may be dictated by grammar, logic, or cadence and is analogous to the pause for breath at the close of a musical phrase. "Every nice ear", wrote Pope, "must, I believe, have observed that in any smooth English verse of ten syllables, there is naturally a pause either at the fourth, fifth, or sixth syllable." Such a pause is a **medial cesura;** if the cesura occurs after another syllable it is a **variant.** Experiments have shown that readers tend to pause after the fourth or sixth syllable in reading blank verse. The cesura is masculine if it occurs after a stressed syllable; the cesura is feminine when occurring after an unstressed syllable. They are illustrated respectively in the first and third lines quoted below. Pope held that the medial cesura should not occur at the same place for more than three successive lines. His skill in shifting it was remarkable, as witness this passage:

> Whether the nymph || shall break Diana's law,
> Or some frail China jar || receive a flaw;
> Or stain her honour || or her new brocade;
> Forget her pray'rs, || or miss a masquerade
> Or lose her heart, || or necklace, || at a ball;
> Or whether Heav'n has doom'd || that Shock must fall.

chanson de geste   An old French epic dealing with actual or legendary events in the early history of France. *The Song of Roland* is the most famous example.

chant royal   See **ballade**, page 17.

charm   A spell uttered to invite a blessing, to avoid an evil, or to call down a malediction. In "The Curse" John Donne is at pains to blast circumstantially "Who ever guesses, thinks, or dreams he knowes" who his mistress is. The witches' scene in *Macbeth* offers another familiar example:

> Double, double toil and trouble;
> Fire burn and cauldron bubble.

Burton Raffel has thus translated an Anglo-Saxon "Charm for Bewitched Land":

> Soil, be well again.
> Earth, mother of men,
> Let God fulfill you with food, be ripe
> And fruitful, give us life.

Chaucer stanza   See **stanza**, page 169.

chiasmus   The inversion in a phrase or clause of the order of words in the preceding phrase or clause, as in Samuel Johnson's line: "For we that live to please, must please to live."

choriambics   A classical metre beginning with a trochee and ending with an iamb, each of the three remaining feet consisting of a trochee and an iamb. Swinburne imitated it in a poem of that title, as did Rupert Brooke, two of whose lines are quoted here:

> Hēre thĕ / flāme thăt wăs āsh, / shrīne thăt wăs vōid, /
>   lōst ĭn thĕ hāunt / ĕd wōod,
> Ī havĕ / tēndĕd ănd lōved, / yēar ŭpŏn yēar, /
>   Ī ĭn thĕ sól / ĭtūde . . .

cinquain   A form invented by Adelaide Crapsey and so called because it consists of five lines, which are of two, four, six, eight, and two syllables respectively. It is an American equivalent of the Japanese haiku or tanka. The example below, by the originator of the form, is called "Triad":

> These be
> Three silent things:
> The falling snow . . . the hour
> Before the dawn . . . the mouth of one
> Just dead.

classical   Having the characteristics of the poetry of ancient Greece and Rome. The adjective is used both of the work of the pre-Christian poets and of later verse believed to resemble it because of the writer's objectivity in the choice and handling of his theme, the clarity and simplicity of his style, the formal structure of the poem, and its restrained tone. **Neo-classical** describes the work of certain early eighteenth-century poets, also known as the Augustans—among whom Pope was the most prominent—who deliberately imitated the ancients. His own lines indicate his models:

> Hear how learn'd Greece her useful rules indites,
> When to repress, and when indulge our flights:
> High on Parnassus' top her sons she show'd,
> And pointed out those arduous paths they trod;
> Held from afar, aloft, th' immortal prize,
> And urg'd the rest by equal steps to rise.
> Just precepts thus from great examples giv'n,
> She drew from them what they deriv'd from Heav'n.

Yvor Winters, a contemporary poet, wrote with classical restraint, as in these lines on the passion that "is the scholar's heritage":

> The passion to condense from book to book
> Unbroken wisdom in a single look,
> Though we know well that when this fix the head,
> The mind's immortal, but the man is dead.

Another such is Robert Frost, with his reasonableness and reserve, his affectionate concern, tinged with irony, for what he knew, his conviction that it is the part of wisdom to

> choose something like a star
> To stay our minds on and be staid.

Awareness of his links with the past, the exercise of discipline and restraint, testify to the classicism to which T. S. Eliot repeatedly paid tribute.

See also **classical prosody; romantic.**

classical hexameter   See **hexameter.** See also **metre,** page 88.

classical prosody   That employed by the ancient Greeks and Romans. See also **metre**, page 88.

clerihew   A form of light verse, originated by Edmund Clerihew Bentley, which in two couplets touches off some well-known character whose name furnishes one of the rhymes. The term is sometimes applied to pieces longer than a quatrain. The first example below is by the originator.

> John Stuart Mill,
> By a mighty effort of will,
> Overcame his natural bonhomie
> And wrote 'Principles of Political Economy'.

> Edmund Clerihew Bentley
> Worked swiftly if not gently,
> Tracking murderers down by a hidden clew
> In whodunit and clerihew.

closed couplet   See **couplet**.

C.M.   Abbreviation for COMMON MEASURE.

common measure   The quatrain a^4 b^3 c^4 b^3 of the ballad stanza, but distinguished from it in being associated with the strict iambics and the exact rhymes found in the hymnal, and so also known as the **hymnal stanza**. This sometimes rhymes a b a b. Its difference from the ballad stanza is apparent if one contrasts the opening quatrain of "Sir Patrick Spens" with the opening stanza of a hymn in C.M.

> The king sits in Dumferling toune,
>   Drinking the blue-reid wine;
> "O whar will I get a guid sailor,
>   To sail this schip of mine?"

> With joy we hail the sacred day

Which God hath called His own;
With joy the summons we obey
To worship at His throne.

Another form of the hymnal stanza is the **short measure or S.M.**,
of which the scheme may be either $a\ b^3\ a^4\ b^3$ or $a\ b^3\ c^4\ b^3$. The
long measure, or **L.M.**, of the hymnal employs either of these
rhyme schemes, but all four lines are iambic tetrameter. C.M.,
as well as L.M. and S.M., may be doubled to form an eight-line
stanza. **Common particular measure** is the name of a six-line
stanza with four feet in the first, second, fourth, and fifth lines,
three feet in the third and sixth. **Short particular measure** is a
stanza having three feet in the first, second, fourth, and fifth
lines, four feet in the third and sixth. Emily Dickinson, who did
not always follow a strict rhyme scheme, employed several of
these stanzas.

common rhythm   See **rhythm**, page 144.

compensation   The means of repairing omissions in a line of
metrical verse. These omissions are usually one or more unstressed syllables though they may also be a whole foot. A syllable omitted in one foot may be added to another to repair the
loss. Occasionally a loss in one line is compensated for in the
next, but it is more usual to find compensation occurring within
the line, as in an example from Pope. It may be scanned as having the five iambs normal in such decasyllabic verse. But it seems
more acceptable to scan it so that the fourth foot is a tribrach,
the additional unstressed syllable there compensating for its
omission in the fifth foot:

The glance / by day, / the whis / per in the / dark . . .

Another form of compensation is the use of a PAUSE other than
the cesura; it may be a **rest** or a hold. The **rest**, analogous to that

in music, is a silence with a temporal value in the metrical scheme. It is apparent in two anapestic lines by Tennyson:

> ˄Break, / ˄break, / ˄break,
> At the foot / of thy crags, / O Sea! ˄

The pause in the last foot of the second line is made more emphatic because the words conclude the line and the poem as well. A long pause is sometimes called a **metrical pause**. The pause that is the result of dwelling upon a syllable is called a **hold**, and is analogous to the hold in music. A line of Kipling's illustrates its use:

> Thûs / sāid thĕ / Lôrd / in thĕ /
> Vāult ā / bōve thĕ / Chērŭ / bim, ˄

The pauses on the first and fourth syllables may be interpreted as rests, but are more easily read as holds. The prolongation of a syllable does not always count, as it does here, in the timing of the metrical line. In such cases the hold is not a compensatory device. It should be remembered that syllables presumed equal to one another have proved not to be so when utterance was timed under laboratory conditions and that experiments have shown the feet in a line of verse to be only approximately equal. The compensation that satisfies the demands of the metrical pattern is therefore apt to differ from that which obtains in the reading of a line, even when the poet is a scrupulous metrist and the reader has a good ear. The balancing of sounds and silences follows a more elastic system than conventional scansion admits.

Gascoigne recognized this when he wrote that though Chaucer's lines "are not always of one selfe same number of Syllables, yet, beyng redde by one that hath understanding, the longest verse, and that which hath most Syllables in it, will fall (to the eare) correspondent unto that whiche hath fewest sillables in it: and like wise that whiche hath in it fewest syllables shalbe founde yet to consist of woordes that have suche naturall sounde, as may seeme equall in length to a verse which hath many moe sillables of lighter accentes". See also **substitution.**

complex metaphor   See **metaphor,** page 82.

conceit   An ingenious, logically complicated image, in which, occasionally, in Dr. Johnson's familiar phrase, "the most hetero-geneous ideas are yoked by violence together"; but which, when effective, as he also says, "if . . . far-fetched" is "worth the car-riage." A conceit may be fancifully elaborated to the point of absurdity, as in the first quotation, from Crashaw, on Mary Magdalene's tears; or it may be superficially incongruous but intrinsic to the poem's meaning, as in the second quotation, from Donne's "A Valediction: Forbidding Mourning".

> And now where'er he strays,
> Among the Galilean mountains,
> Or more unwelcome ways,
> He's follow'd by two faithful fountains;
> Two walking baths; two weeping motions;
> Portable, and compendious oceans.

> If they be two, they are two so
>   As stiffe twin compasses are two,
> Thy soule the fixt foot, makes no show
>   To move, but doth, if th' other doe.

> And though it in the center sit,
>   Yet when the other far doth rome,
> It leanes, and hearkens after it,
>   And growes erect, as that comes home.

> Such wilt thou be to mee, who must
>   Like th' other foot, obliquely runne;

> Thy firmnes drawes my circle just,
> And makes me end, where I begunne.

concrete particular   See **concrete universal.**

concrete poetry   substitutes for such conventional elements
of the poem as metre, rhyme, stanzaic form, and even normal
syntax, the ultimate elements of language: letter, syllable, word,
in such a constellation that the visual effect of the typography,
which may be in color, is of an importance equal or superior
to that of the semantic and phonetic elements involved. Although its composition became an international movement in
the Fifties, concrete poetry goes back to the ancients, and more
recent examples of it or close approximations to it may be
found in George Herbert's poem printed in the shape of an
altar, in Apollinaire's CALLIGRAMMES, in the poems of Dylan
Thomas's "Vision and Prayer", shaped like a diamond or womb,
an hour-glass or chalice, and in much of E. E. Cummings' work.
Concrete poetry would have been appreciated by the Chinese
professor who told Frédéric O'Brady that poetry means nothing
to the blind, since "the beauty of the written page is the beauty
of the poem itself". The professor was referring, of course, to
Chinese calligraphy, yet by the same token, for the concrete
poet, the beauty of his work lies in its patent manifestation.
William Jay Smith's "typewriter poems" are only tangential to
the genre, since they serve as illustrations to the accompanying
verses. May Swenson's typographical games are closer approximations to it. Some poems are concrete in the physical sense.
Thus, Ian Hamilton Finlay constructed "The Horizon of Holland" with the notion that "the horizon of Holland is all ears".
The letters of "all" and "ears", painted blue, were distributed
along paired 6′ yellowish arms thrusting up from a 15′ horizontal
strip, to suggest the arms (or "ears") of windmills. He calls these
constructs "poem-objects". Another concrete poet, Mathias

Goeritz, has sculptured monumental poems, constellated of a single word or a single letter in iron. Some authors are chiefly concerned with linguistics, others are mathematically oriented. When an ideogram does not constitute a concrete poem, it may naturally be a prominent feature of such a poem. Words or letters may undergo permutation and superposition. A poem by Claus Bremer presents the repeated phrase: "rendering the legible illegible" (English translation), and by increasing superposition creates precisely this effect—which sometimes occurs unintentionally elsewhere. Occasionally a composition depends largely on its aural values. Poems may also be games, or wholly the result of chance. Metaphysically inclined poets' compositions offer a play on words whose meanings proliferate so that they demand exegesis. There are pieces in which the significance of allusions, associations, and implications combine with the pictorial or structural nature of the poem to make for maximum effectiveness. The reader may be invited to participate in a poem by his way of reading it, in the literal sense of the phrase. The creator of the concrete poem, largely through manoeuvring typography, is intent upon achieving an immediacy often lost in even the freer modes of conventional poems.

concrete universal　　A term taken over from philosophy to signify a poem wherein an ideal organization—that may be the poet's idea of the world or may be his intellectual ordering of an experience—by means of the choice and the formal arrangement of words takes on the actuality of what is seen, heard, tasted, touched, and felt. In "Tintern Abbey" the universal is Wordsworth's pantheistic philosophy, but it requires

> the light of setting suns,
> And the round ocean, and the living air,
> And the blue sky, . . .

saluted by a poet who was

> A lover of the meadow and the woods,
> And mountains; and of all that we behold
> From this green earth; of all the mighty world
> Of eye, and ear,—both what they half create,
> And what perceive; . . .

as the poem bodies them forth in detail, to make that universal a concrete one. Each detail is a **concrete particular.** This may be a sight such as astronomers observed and Coleridge presented in his lines about

> The horned Moon, with one bright star
> Within the nether tip.

It may be something as unreal as Kubla Khan's palace, erected in the poet's mind, by his own account, with the help of an opiate, yet definitely delineated in his poem: "A sunny pleasure-dome with caves of ice!"

confessional poetry   Most lyrics are such, being expressive of intimate personal feelings, but the term has come to be associated with poems about private experience extraordinarily mean, ugly, or harrowing—and not unrelated to the public horrors of life in our time. James Dickey points out that confessional poetry differs from lyric in that the former involves exorcism. This is not true of the song in which Samuel Daniel declares: "Love is a sickness full of woes", nor even of Poe's unhappy admission: "From childhood's hour I have not been / As others were— . . .". It is true of poems dealing boldly with the author's mental illness or with extreme disaffection. Such is Robert Lowell's "Waking Early Sunday Morning", in which he sees above the fog the white spire and the white flag-pole sticking out "like old white china doorknobs, sad/slight useless things to calm the mad". Such is Sylvia Plath's "Lady Lazarus", the survivor of several suicide attempts, her skin "Bright as a

Nazi lampshade". Such are some of John Berryman's *Dream Songs*, with their black humor, and the naked pathos of their colloquial avowals, as in the line, "I'm scared a only one thing, which is me."

connotation   Any meaning suggested by the sound or the look of a word or associated, however remotely, with its usual specific meaning. **Denotation** is the accepted meaning of a word. The connotations of language thicken its ambiguities and also give it greater emotional weight, so that they may enrich its value for the poet. The pun is vulgar to the vulgus; its many-faceted sparkle has always delighted the poet, from Shakespeare to Richard Wilbur. The King, addressing Hamlet as "my son", is interrupted with, "A little more than kin, and less than kind". The implication of "less than kind" is at once that the King is cruel and that his fatherly relationship to Hamlet is unlawful. Similarly, when Wilbur speaks of heavy nuns who "walk in a pure floating / Of dark habits", the pun gives greater depth to the picture.

The symbolists relied largely on the connotative aspect of language. Hart Crane, one of their American followers, evokes all the associations of music along with the motion of a boat coasting in an archipelago in the single phrase, "Adagios of islands".

The imagists, seeking the accurate word, were not relying simply upon its denotation. William Carlos Williams begins a poem thus:

> This is the time of year
> when boys fifteen and seventeen
> wear two horned lilac blossoms
> in their caps—or over one ear

The language seems uncomplicated. Yet the word "horned" carries connotations of fauns and satyrs far from the American suburbs that the poem clearly presents.

The self-styled activist aims to make the fullest possible use of the connotations of both sounds and imagery. Rosalie Moore, in a poem dedicated to Hopkins, uses the phrase "pierced insects of sight". Our glimpses of the world are, like insects, small and fleeting. "Pierced insects" presents an image of mounted moths. The phrase as a whole suggests precious glimpses fixed in the memory. "Pierced" also connotes a painfully intense experience, and especially the crucifixion which had supreme significance for the Jesuit poet to whom the lines are addressed. He himself coined the word "inscape" to mean the intrinsic, self-expressive quality of a thing. "Insect", in this context, recalls "inscape" and also reminds us of the segmented, fractional character of our insights. These connotations are to some degree supported by the dry sound of the words. See also **ambiguity; symbol; verbal texture.**

consonance   See **rhyme**, page 131.

consonantal assonance   See **rhyme**, page 131.

consonantal dissonance   See **rhyme**, page 131.

consonantal rhyme   See **rhyme**, page 131.

counterpoint   The term used by Gerald Manley Hopkins for a line of verse in which two scansions coexist, SPRUNG RHYTHM being "mounted" on the formal metre. He cites as examples the choruses of *Samson Agonistes*. The following passage, with two heroic lines and the recurrent iambic foot, is illustrative:

> For him I reckon not in high estate
> Whom long descent of birth
> Or the sphear of fortune raises;
> But thee whose strength, while virtue was her mate,

> Might have subdu'd the Earth,
> Universally crown'd with highest praises.

couplet   Two lines of verse, usually in the same metre and joined by rhyme, that form a unit. A closed couplet is one that is logically or grammatically complete, such as Pope's

> Instruct the planets in what orbs to run,
> Correct old Time, and regulate the Sun; . . .

Both lines are **end-stopped**: each has a logical pause at its close. The first line of a couplet is said to be run-on when the sense runs over to the succeeding line. This is also called **enjambment.** A closed couplet rarely exhibits enjambment but it may do so, as these lines by the same poet bear witness:

> In that blest moment from his oozy bed
> Old father Thames advanc'd his reverend head.

An **open couplet** is one in which the second line is run-on and requires the first line of the succeeding couplet to complete its meaning. It was used by Milton in these lines:

> Look in, and see each blissful Deitie
> How he before the thunderous thron doth lie,
> Listening to what unshorn *Apollo* sings
> To th' touch of golden wires, while *Hebe* brings
> Immortal Nectar to her Kingly Sire: . . .

The masters of the HEROIC COUPLET relieved its monotony in various ways. One of them was the introduction of a triplet, three lines on the same rhyme, the last line occasionally being an alexandrine, as in this example from Dryden:

> Thy gen'rous Fruits, though gather'd ere their prime,
> Still shew'd a Quickness; and maturing Time
> But mellows what we write to the dull Sweets of Rhyme.

The **short couplet** is in tetrameter, and may be iambic or trochaic.

This example is from Milton:

> And ever against eating Cares,
> Lap me in soft *Lydian* Aires,
> Married to immortal verse
> Such as the meeting soul may pierce
> In notes, with many a winding bout
> Of lincked sweetness long drawn out, . . .

The short couplet is sometimes called octosyllabic because each line is composed of eight syllables. This is true of the passage quoted above if "Married" is pronounced as a word of three syllables, "lincked" as a word of two syllables, and "many a" is slurred to form two syllables. Later poets took increasing liberties with the couplet, as witness these passages from Keats, Kipling, and Auden:

> What is more tranquil than a musk-rose blowing
> In a green island, far from all men's knowing?
> More healthful than the leafiness of dales?
> More secret than a nest of nightingales?

> More serene than Cordelia's countenance?
> More full of Vision than a high romance?
> What, but thee, Sleep? Soft closer of men's eyes!
> Low murmurer of tender lullabies.

> Churning an' choking and chuckling, quiet and scummy
>   and dark—
> Full to her lower hatches and risin' steady. Hark!

> You in the town now call the exile fool
> That writes home once a year as last leaves fall,

> Think—Romans had a language in their day
> And ordered roads with it, but it had to die: . . .

cross-rhyme   See **Welsh forms**, page 190.

crossed rhyme   See **rhyme**, page 131.

cubist poetry   Heterogeneous images and statements, presented in a seemingly disordered but considered fashion, so that together they build a coherent work. It answers to Picasso's description of a painting as "a sum of destructions", with the emphasis upon "sum". Like a cubist canvas, such poetry breaks down the elements of an experience in order to create a new synthesis and so represent it more truly. Memorable poems of this kind were composed by Guillaume Apollinaire, whose influence is discoverable in the work of MacLeish, Cummings, and Kenneth Rexroth. A fragment from one of Rexroth's poems will indicate the method:

> As speaks the celeste
> As speaks the ineffable triangle
> The note which could never be interrupted and would never stop
> O merle. O. O. O. O. O. O.
> The gnomon falls erratic on the tangled thicket
> The odor of raspberries crushed in the hot sun

Cummings follows the method of cubism in destroying the sequence of syllables and the logic of punctuation so that the fragments compose an evocative whole, as in these lines:

>   when
>   sunbeams loot
> furnished rooms through whose foul windows absurd
> clouds cruise nobly ridiculous skies

(the;mselve;s a;nd scr;a;tch-ing lousy full.of.rain
beggars yaw:nstretchy:awn)
                              then,
                                      o my love
                                              , then

it's Spring

curtal sonnet   See sonnet, page 161.

cynghanedd   See rhyme, page 131; **Welsh forms**, page 190.

[D]

dactyl A foot of three syllables, the first long or stressed, the other two short or unstressed. See also **metre**, page 88.

dactylic See **metre**, page 88.

dead metaphor See **metaphor**, page 82.

decasyllabic verse Lines composed of ten syllables. Milton's *Paradise Lost* is one of the best exemplars of the variety that it affords, as witness two lines:

> Created hugest that swim th' Ocean stream
>
> The Birds thir quire apply; aires, vernal aires

decorum Suiting the manner to the matter, be it high, middle, or low, a virtue demanded of the poet by Elizabethan rhetoricians. The decent sobriety that we associate with the term was therefore held suitable to subjects for which the middle style was appropriate. Satiric verse required the low style, which sets forth the matter plainly in common words, so that by antipoetic forthrightness the poet kept decorum. As Puttenham recognized, "neither is all that may be written of Kings and Princes such as ought to keepe a high stile, nor all that may be written upon a shepheard to keepe the low, but according to the matter reported". These considerations bear upon the tone of the speaker, and so upon the attitude that dictates it. The writers who were enjoined to observe

decorum, like their mentors, held that poetry was one means
of discovering the order of the universe. Their view of it is
expressed in Ulysses' speech in *Troilus and Cressida*, some lines
of which follow:

> The heavens themselves, the planets, and this centre,
> Observe degree, priority and place,
> Insisture, course, proportion, season, form,
> Office and custom, in all line of order; . . .
> . . . O, when degree is shaked,
> Which is the ladder of all high designs,
> The enterprise is sick! How could communities,
> Degrees in schools and brotherhoods in cities,
> Peaceful commerce from dividable shores,
> The primogenitive and due of birth,
> Prerogative of age, crowns, sceptres, laurels,
> But by degree, stand in authentic place?
> Take but degree away, untune that string,
> And, hark, what discord follows!

denotation   See **connotation.**

didactic verse   That which aims to teach. Verse concerned
with instruction rather than with imaginative understanding
borders more nearly upon prose than upon poetry. Often satirical, it loses much of its interest when the object of satire retreats
into the shades of religious, political, or social history. John
Manifold upholds it characteristically in didactic lines on the
art of verse in which he speaks of

> that best reward the poet needs—
> To know his Words result in worthy Deeds.

Dr. Johnson gave Juvenal's Tenth Satire a didactic emphasis
absent from the original, as in the admonition:

> Yet hope not life from grief or danger free,
> Nor think the doom of man reversed for thee.

dimeter   See **metre**, page 88. See also **measure**.

dipody   See **measure**.

dirge   See **elegy**.

dissociation of sensibility   See **sensibility**.

dissonance   See **rhyme**, page 131.

dissyllabic foot   A foot of two syllables. See **metre**, page 88.

distich   A couplet. The former term is often reserved for the couplet used in classical elegiacs.

distributed stress   The effect produced when it is doubtful which of two consecutive syllables takes the stress. Since the stress or accent appears to hover over both syllables, it is also called **hovering accent**. It may occur because the poet was the victim of what Chaucer called

> so greet diversitee,
> In English and in wryting of our tonge,

or it may be a deliberate device. In the following line Milton used distributed stress to create a lingering effect:

> Now came still Eevning on, and Twilight gray . . .

dithyramb   A lyric, vehement in tone and irregular in structure, suggesting the character of the choric hymn to Dionysus which was the original Greek meaning of the word.

doggerel   Trivial, badly written verse that is sometimes intentionally, more often, like the lines below, unintentionally, humorous:

The poor Ass staggered with the shock;
And then, as if to take his ease,
In quiet uncomplaining mood,
Upon the spot where he had stood,
Dropped gently down upon his knees;

As gently on his side he fell;
And by the river's brink did lie;
And, while he lay like one that mourned,
The patient Beast on Peter turned
His shining hazel eye.

'Twas but one mild, reproachful look,
A look more tender than severe;
And straight in sorrow, not in dread,
He turned the eye-ball in his head
Towards the smooth river deep and clear.

WORDSWORTH

double ballade   See **ballade**, page 17.

double dactyl   is the name of a tricky form invented by
Anthony Hecht, consisting of two quatrains, the first three lines
of which are two dactyls, the fourth a dactyl and a macron.
The last line of the poem rhymes with the fourth. The first
line is nonsense, "Higgledy-piggledy" being frequently used.
The second line, suggestive of the far less elaborate CLERIHEW,
is a proper name. Titles are permissible, such as "Admiral
Morison", and epithets if often accompanying the name, such
as "Jupiter Pluvius". One double dactyllic line, preferably the
penultimate one, consists of a single word. Each use of such a
word precludes its introduction into any subsequent double
dactyl. Foreign languages are allowable; indeed, the inventor
has expressed the hope "that this will restore macaronic verse

to the dignity it has not enjoyed since the Middle Ages." An
example follows:

> Fiddlety-diddlety
> Hecht atque Hollander,
> Didacts and wits with a
> Soupçon of Sade,
>
> Made of the form that the
> Former invented an
> UltraDraconian
> Joke on the *fade*.

double rhyme   See **rhyme**, page 131.

duple rhythm   See **rhythm**, page 144.

[E]

eclogue   See **pastoral.**

elegiac pentameter   See **pentameter.**

elegiacs   Used for dirges by the Greeks and Romans, this verse form consists of a distich, the first line being a classical hexameter, the second an elegiac pentameter. Schiller's descriptive couplet imitating it has been translated into English by several poets, among them Longfellow:

So the Hexameter, rising and singing, with cadence sonorous,
    Falls, and in refluent rhythm back the Pentameter flows.

They are appropriately if not impeccably used by E. A. Robinson in "Pasa Thalassa Thalassa", as this distich indicates:

Down with a twittering flash go the smooth and
    inscrutable swallows,
Down to the place made theirs by the cold work of
    the sea.

elegy   A poem of lament or of grave meditation. The term was at one time applied to a work, on any subject, composed in the ELEGIACS used in Greek and Roman poems of mourning. A later meaning was a poem, whatever the metre, in which the writer meditated upon his sentiments. The type is illustrated by Gray's "Elegy in a Country Churchyard", Shelley's "Adonais",

Yeats's "In Memory of Major Robert Gregory". Auden's
"Elegy for J.F.K.", which bears the date (November 22, 1963)
of Kennedy's death, is of technical interest as well as being
otherwise memorable. Each of the four stanzas is in the form
of a haiku, composed of 17 syllables. These are the first and
last stanzas:

> Why *then*, why *there*,
> Why *thus*, we cry, did he die?
> The heavens are silent.
>
> When a just man dies,
> Lamentation and praise,
> Sorrow and joy, are one.

An example which, in the original German and in English
translation, has had a wide influence on contemporary poets is
Rainer Maria Rilke's *Duino Elegies*. Rilke mourns neither the
humble dead consigned to forgotten graves nor yet any memorable and beloved person. The *Duino Elegies* are the lament
of unearthly powers over human weakness in penetrating and
transfiguring reality. Edna St. Vincent Millay prefaced a group
of lyrics addressed to a dead schoolmate with the quatrain:

> Oh, loveliest of all sweet throats,
> Where now no more the music is,
> With hands that wrote you little notes,
> I write you little elegies!

One of these poems was entitled "Dirge". The dirge and the
threnody are songs of lamentation that are apt to be less meditative than the elegy and more poignant. See also **pastoral**.

elision   The omission of an unstressed syllable in order to
make the line conform to the metrical scheme. Milton made

notable use of elision in his blank verse, though he tended to slur the unnecessary syllable rather than to excise it. The following lines are illustrative:

> O're many a Frozen, many a fierie Alpe,
> Rocks, Caves, Lakes, Fens, Bogs, Dens, and shades of
>   death,
> A Universe of death, which God by curse
> Created evil, for evil only good . . .

If the final and initial vowels in "many a" and "fierie Alpe" are slurred, the first line may be read as iambic pentameter. The same line offers another type of elision, in which a syllable is cut out of the middle of a word: "O're" for "over". In the fourth line the word "evil" is elided before "only". **Synalepha** is the name given to elision when two syllables have adjacent vowels of which one is suppressed, as in Pope's "And strike to dust th' imperial tow'rs of Troy". See also **metre**.

embryonic rhyme   See **rhyme**, page 131.

end-rhyme   See **rhyme**, page 131.

end-stopped line   See **couplet**, page 38.

English sonnet   See **sonnet**, page 161.

englyn   See **Welsh forms**, page 190.

enjambment   See **couplet**.

envelope   See **stanza**, page 169.

envoy   See **ballade**.

epic   A narrative poem, noble in conception and style, which treats of a series of heroic exploits or significant events and usually centers upon the adventures and accomplishments of one hero, such as Odysseus in the *Odyssey*. The word is also used adjectivally to describe both such poems and characteristics of the epic found elsewhere. Hardy's quasi-dramatic poem *The Dynasts* is one of the few works by a poet of our own time that has an epic sweep.

epigram   A short and usually pointed poem. Such is Donne's couplet:

> Thy flattering picture, *Phryne,* is like thee,
> Onely in this, that you both painted be.

epistle   A letter in verse. Theme and tone in such poems vary almost as much as in prose letters. Burns begins an "Epistle to a Young Friend":

> I lang hae thought, my youthfu' friend,
>   A something to have sent you,
> Tho' it should serve nae ither end
>   Than just a kind memento;
> But how the subject theme may gang,
>   Let time and change determine;
> Perhaps it may turn out a sang,
>   Perhaps turn out a sermon.

Donne mixed sermon and song in his epistles. These lines commence one of several that he addressed to Sir Henry Wotton:

> Sir, more than kisses, letters mingle Soules;
> For, thus friends absent speake. This ease controules
> The tediousness of my life: But for these   .
> I could ideate nothing, which could please,
> But I should wither in one day, and passe
> To'a bottle'of Hay, that am a locke of grasse.

Auden composed a *Letter to Lord Byron,* of nearly 40 pages, in rhyme royal, of which this stanza gives the character:

Byron, thou should'st be living at this hour!
        What would you do, I wonder, if you were?
Britannia's lost prestige and cash and power,
        Her middle classes show some wear and tear,
        We've learned to bomb each other from the air;
I can't imagine what the Duke of Wellington
        Would say about the music of Duke Ellington.

epitaph   A short poem to be inscribed on a tomb or in imitation of such commemorative lines. It is not always in pious
praise of the dead; witness this by Burns on a schoolmaster:

> Here lie Willie Michie's banes;
>   O Satan, when ye tak him,
> Gie him the schoolin' of your weans,
>   For clever deils he'll mak them!

epithalamion   A nuptial poem, of which the most famous
example is Spenser's, composed to celebrate his second marriage.
The last of the twenty-three stanzas invokes the blessings of the
gods, "That we may raise a large posterity", and a noble one,
concluding:

> So let us rest, sweet love, in hope of this,
> And cease till then our tymely joys to sing:
> The woods no more us answer, nor our eccho ring.

In a coda he asks that his song may be "a goodly ornament" to
his bride "And for short time an endless moniment". And so
it has, for not so short a time. Spenser was responsible for the
term **"prothalamion"**, used of a poem composed before the
celebration of a wedding. He furnished a memorable example
in that which bears the refrain: "Sweet Thames! run softly,
till I end my song." It is usual for a nuptial song to be of some
length, meditative rather than ecstatic, and written by a friend

of the chief actors in the ceremony. The range of these poems
varies greatly however. John Peale Bishop commemorated his
wedding night in two quatrains entitled "Epithalamium" (a
variant spelling). In wartime Auden wrote an "Epithalamion"
which begins

> While explosives blow to dust
> Friends and hopes, we cannot pray, . . .

but went on to plead:

> May this bed of marriage be
> Symbol now of the rebirth
> Asked of old humanity; . . . .

epode   See **ode**, page 107.

equivalence   See **substitution**.

etymological accent   See **accent**.

even accent   See **accent**.

extrametrical syllable   See **catalectic**.

eye rhyme   See **rhyme**, page 131.

[F]

falling rhythm   See **rhythm**, page 144.

fancy   The faculty of using imagery in a novel and often arbitrary way that is without great significance. It means also such an image or CONCEIT. Jonson displays Fancy in more senses than one when he brings her on stage and gives her these words:

> And Fancy, I tell you, has dreams that have wings,
> And dreams that have honey, and dreams that have stings,
> Dreams of the maker, and dreams of the teller,
> Dreams of the kitchen, and dreams of the cellar;
> Some that are tall, and some that are dwarfs,
> Some that are haltered, and some that wear scarfs;
> Some that are proper, and signify o' thing,
> And some another, and some that are nothing.

Fancy is here, as often, synonymous with **fantasy**, though that term applies more narrowly to extravagant inventions, as if, to continue Fancy's speech,

> . . . a dream should come in now to make you afeard,
>   With a windmill on's head and bells at his beard.

Fantasy differs from **phantasy**, a visionary power that is above whimsy and goes beyond sensory perceptions. The word spelled in this way is also used of the creatures of that power. Thus Ariel and Caliban may be described either as phantasies or as creations of the poet's phantasy. This is one of the chief evidences of the imaginative faculty. See also **imagination**, page 68.

fantasy   See **fancy.**

feminine ending   An unstressed syllable at the close of a line, as in the third of these lines by Richard Wilbur:

> Let me now rejoice
> In all impostures, take
> The shape of lion or leopard,
> Boar, or watery snake . . .

This is sometimes called a **light ending.** When a line concludes on a stressed syllable, like the others quoted above, it has a **masculine ending.**

feminine rhyme   See **rhyme**, page 131.

figurative language   That in which the literal meaning of words is disregarded in order to show or imply a relationship between diverse things. The relationship is usually one of direct or implied resemblance but may emphasize contrast. Such language is made up of figures of speech. These are also called **tropes.** Traditional rhetoric included a number of tropes. Contemporary criticism of poetry is concerned chiefly with META-PHOR, METONYMY, SYNECDOCHE, and IRONY. See also **ambiguity; symbol.**

foot   See **metre**, page 88. For types of feet commonly used in English verse, see page 93. See also **Ionic; paeon; prosodic symbols.**

form   The metrical and stanzaic organization of a poem. The form may be a conventional one, established by long use, such as the pattern of a ballad, a sonnet, or of any of the FRENCH

FORMS, or the dialogue between herdsmen in a pastoral, a convention that obtains when the sophisticated poet appears in rustic disguise. The form may, however, be as loose and novel as polyphonic prose. R. S. Crane conceives form otherwise, as "that which gives definite shape, emotional power, and beauty to the materials of man's experience out of which the writer has composed his work". For this Aristotelian critic, form is a "synthesizing principle". It therefore suggests **organic form.** This term is used by Herbert Read of a poem that "has its own inherent laws, originating with its very invention and fusing in one vital unity both structure and content . . ." Hopkins' successful experiments in sprung rhythm are an instance of this, but one also finds it in traditional poems where theme, structure, and texture are integrated. A sonnet by Wordsworth illustrating the lack of organic form begins:

> A genial hearth, a hospitable board,
> And a refined rusticity, belong
> To the neat mansion, where, his flock among,
> The learned Pastor dwells, their watchful Lord.

Its presence is exemplified in another sonnet by the same hand:

> Where lies the Land to which yon Ship must go?
> Fresh as a lark mounting at break of day,
> Festively she puts forth in trim array;
> Is she for tropic suns, or polar snow?
> What boots the enquiry?—Neither friend nor foe
> She cares for; let her travel where she may,
> She finds familiar names, a beaten way
> Ever before her, and a wind to blow.
> Yet still I ask, what haven is her mark?
> And, almost as it was when ships were rare,
> (From time to time, like Pilgrims, here and there
> Crossing the waters) doubt, and something dark,

> Of the old Sea some reverential fear,
>   Is with me at thy farewell, joyous Bark!

Structure is another term for the formal aspect of a poem. When not synonymous with form, as defined above, it means the arrangement and development of images, metaphors, statements, and situations in relation to the theme. Cleanth Brooks equates structure with what he calls "a coherent and powerful" organization of "attitudes" by poetic strategies. The **logical structure** of a poem is revealed in a concise prose paraphrase of its argument. See also **texture**.

fourteener   See **metre**, page 88. See also **poulter's measure**.

free verse   As the term implies, this form does not obey the rules of metrical verse. It demands of those who use it and those who would enjoy it a sensitiveness to what its practitioners call **cadences**. These are phrases which fall into the symmetrical or nearly symmetrical pattern observed when speech rhythm is highly organized. Such symmetry approaches the balance of phrases in a musical composition. Indeed, when it was hard for free verse to win friends and influence poets, one of its champions told apprentices to the craft of poetry that they should "compose in the sequence of the musical phrase, not in the sequence of the metronome", and later, à propos of free verse, quoted Couperin's remark that clavecin players tended to confuse measure, which defines the number and equality of beats, with cadence, which is "properly the spirit, the soul that must be added". Free verse is a literal translation of *vers libre*, which flourished in France in the eighties of the last century. There it meant the freeing of verse from such laws of French prosody as the assignment of a given place to the cesura and the counting of lines as equal if they had the same number of syllables, these and further relaxations resulting in a fluidity of form that easily expressed the temper of the poet. Because of

the differences between the two languages, notably the fact that
words are not accented in French as they are in English, similar
prosodic liberties have diverse effects, so that free verse here and
in England seemed even more of a break with tradition than
did *vers libre* in France. Its adherents have called attention to
the fact that it had been practiced by masters who had not
heard its name. They adduced the work of Milton, Dryden,
Blake, Arnold, Henley, and Whitman. Passages from the work
of some of these poets and that of twentieth-century writers of
free verse will illustrate its nature.

> Oh how comely it is and how reviving
> To the Spirits of just men long opprest!
> When God into the hands of thir deliverer
> Puts invincible might
> To quell the mighty of the Earth, th' oppressour,
> The brute and boist'rous force of violent men
> Hardy and industrious to support
> Tyrannic power, but raging to pursue
> The righteous and all such as honour Truth;
> He all thir Ammunition
> And feats of War defeats
> With plain Heroic magnitude of mind
> And celestial vigour arm'd,
>
>   MILTON

> And you, ye stars!
> Who slowly begin to marshal,
> As of old, in the fields of heaven,
> Your distant, melancholy lines—
> Have you, too, survived yourselves?
> Are you, too, what I fear to become?
> You too once lived—
> You too moved joyfully

Among august companions
In an older world, peopled by Gods,
In a mightier order,
The radiant, rejoicing, intelligent Sons of Heaven!

ARNOLD

Now I am terrified at the Earth, it is that calm and
    patient,
It grows such sweet things out of such corruption,
It turns harmless and stainless on its axis, with such
    endless succession of diseas'd corpses,
It distills such exquisite winds out of such infused fetor,
It renews with such unwitting looks its prodigal, annual,
    sumptuous crops,
It gives such divine materials to men, and accepts such
    leavings from them at last.

WHITMAN

In the far South the sun of autumn is passing
Like Walt Whitman walking along a ruddy shore.
He is singing and chanting the things that are part of him,
The words that were and will be, death and day.
Nothing is final, he chants. No man shall see the end.
His beard is of fire and his staff is a leaping flame.

STEVENS

See, they return; ah, see the tentative
Movements, and the slow feet,
The trouble in the pace and the uncertain
Wavering.

See, they return, one, and by one,
With fear, as half-awakened;
As if the snow should hesitate

> And murmur in the wind,
>   and half turn back;
> These were the "Wing'd-with-Awe",
>   Inviolable.

POUND

Although strict form is by definition foreign to free verse, its rhythms can often be characterized in terms appropriate to metrical verse. A poem in free verse by John Gould Fletcher may therefore be said to have a dactylic rhythm proper to the image of galloping forms that it presents:

> Over the roof-tops race the shadows of clouds;
> Like horses the shadows of clouds charge down the street.

Similarly, the movement of these lines by H. D. is spondaic:

> we met
> but one god,
> one tall god with a spear-shaft,
> one bright god with a lance.

See also **polyphonic prose; projective verse; sprung rhythm.**

French forms   Ingenious and elaborate lyrical patterns that originated with the troubadours of Provence and were imported into English verse in Chaucer's time. Several of these patterns were used with supreme effectiveness by the French master François Villon in the fifteenth century, and it was largely on his work that the Victorians and their successors modeled their imitations. The forms chiefly used in English verse included the various types of the BALLADE and the RONDEAU, as well as the SESTINA and the VILLANELLE. See also **pantoum; virelay.**

full rhyme   See rhyme, page 131.

functional metaphor   See metaphor, page 82.

[G]

Georgianism   A term for the work of a group of British poets who flourished in the reign of George V and who, with a few notable exceptions, treated the stock themes of lyric poetry in a conventional manner. The first of the Georgian anthologies was issued by Edward Marsh in 1912. In his preface to the final anthology, published in 1923, the editor said that "much admired modern work" seemed to him "in its lack of inspiration and its disregard of form, like gravy imitating lava". He admitted that much of the work that he preferred might seem to others "in its lack of inspiration and its comparative finish, like tapioca imitating pearls". Because many of the Georgian poets wrote as though the industrial revolution had never taken place and affected dowdy literary fashions, Georgianism suggests verse without complexity, power, or freshness. Nevertheless, some admirable work appeared in these anthologies. So careful a craftsman as Wilfred Owen was proud to be "held peer by the Georgians" and Robert Frost was of their company when his first book of poems appeared.

Georgics   Derived from Vergil's *carmina georgica*, songs of husbandry, the term refers to poems dealing with like themes.

gnomic verse   Aphoristic verse, especially that written by certain Greek poets in the sixth and seventh centuries B.C., such as Theognis, the author of these lines, translated by J. H. Frere:

> Waste not your efforts, struggle not, my friend,
> Idle and old abuses to defend:
> Take heed! the very measures that you press
> May bring repentance with their own success.

goliard   A learned vagabond of the middle ages who celebrated the pleasures of the flesh and satirized the selfish beneficiaries of the established order in Latin verse notable for its departure from classical prosody and for the use of rhyme. The self-styled Arch-Poet, otherwise anonymous, is the reputed author of "The Confessions of Golias". This name, scornfully bestowed on Abelard, among others, is associated with the Latin word for gluttony and with Goliath, giant symbol of wickedness. Frost pays tribute to the goliardic poets in lines that recall their songs of spring sprinkling the earth with flowers:

> Yet singing but Dione in the wood
> And *ver aspergit terram floribus*
> They slowly led old Latin verse to rhyme
> And to forget the ancient lengths of time,
> And so began the modern world for us.

Gongorism   An affected style of writing so called after the Spanish poet, Luis de Gongora y Argote, a contemporary of the author of *Euphues*, from which, in 1592, the word "euphuism" came. The sestet from Gongora's sonnet on "The Rose of Life" in Sir Richard Fanshawe's rendering suggests the manner:

> Some clown's coarse lungs will poison thy sweet flower
>   If by the careless plough thou shalt be torn:
>   And many Herods lie in wait each hour
>   To murther thee as soon as thou art born,
> Nay, force thy bud to blow; their tyrant breath,
> Anticipating life, to hasten death.

grammatical accent   See **accent.**

[H]

haiku   A Japanese poem in three lines, of 5, 7, and 5 syllables respectively, which presents a clear picture so as at once to rouse emotion and suggest a spiritual insight. The strict rules governing the form cannot be followed in translation, especially since Japanese is unstressed. This version of a haiku by the sixteenth-century poet Moritake may hint at the structure:

> The falling flower
> I saw drift back to the branch
> Was a butterfly.

The poem refers to the Buddhist proverb that the fallen flower never returns to the branch; the broken mirror never again reflects. A somewhat similar type of Japanese poem is the **tanka**, consisting of five lines, the first and third of which have 5 syllables and the others 7, making 31 syllables in all. Below is a version of a tanka on the death of his little son written by Okura more than a thousand years ago:

> Since he is too young
> To know the way, I would plead:
> "Pray, accept this gift,
> O Underworld messenger,
> And bear the child pick-a-back."

The imagists, notably John Gould Fletcher, imitated the intent if not the form of the haiku, which they spelled HOKKU, and that

of the tanka. A near approach in English to these Japanese
forms is found in Adelaide Crapsey's CINQUAINS. In "For Friends
Only" Auden originates a variant on the tanka in which the
pattern is 7, 5, 7, 5, 7, 5, and relates not to the number of syllables but to the number of words in the line, as this opening
stanza illustrates:

> Ours, yet not ours, being set apart
> As a shrine to friendship,
> Empty and silent most of the year,
> This room awaits from you
> What you alone, as visitor, can bring,
> A weekend of personal life.

More frequently this poet uses a closer approximation to the
haiku, making a poem, or more often a stanza, of 17 words or
17 syllables, but not distributing them in the orthodox fashion.
These lines from the *Postscript* to "The Cave of Nakedness"
exemplify his practice:

> Our bodies cannot love:
> But, without one,
> What works of Love could we do?

half rhyme   See **rhyme**, page 131.

head rhyme   See **rhyme**, page 131.

headless line   See **catalectic**.

hemistich   A half line of verse.

hendecasyllabics   Lines of eleven syllables, but the term
usually refers to the classical pentameter line in which the first
and last feet are trochees or spondees, the second foot a dactyl,

the third and fourth feet trochaic. Tennyson imitated it in the lines beginning:

> Look, I come to the test, a tiny poem
> All composed in a metre of Catullus.

heptameter   A seven-foot line. See also **metre**, page 88.

heroic couplet   See **heroic line.**

heroic line   Iambic pentameter, so called because it was used for heroic or epic poetry in English. When the stanza is of two lines only, it is called a **heroic couplet.** A quatrain in this metre is known as the **heroic stanza.** The heroic line in classical prosody is the HEXAMETER. Verse composed of heroic lines, whether the English pentameter or the classical hexameter, is known as **heroic verse.**

heroic stanza   See **heroic line.**

heroic verse   See **heroic line.**

hexameter   The classical hexameter is a line of six feet, of which the first four may be either dactylic or spondaic, the fifth is a dactyl and the sixth a spondee. Imitations of it in English verse have been frequent and faulty, inevitably tending to substitute stress for quantity and to make the metre monotonously dactylic, so that it seems not to be in 4/4 time but in waltz time. See also **elegiacs; heroic line; metre**, page 88.

historical rhyme   See **rhyme**, page 131.

hokku   See **haiku.**

hold   A pause on a syllable. See also **compensation.**

Horatian ode   See **ode**, page 107.

hovering accent   See **distributed stress.**

Hudibrastic verse   is so-called because of its use in *Hudibras,*
a mock-heroic satire on the Puritans, by Samuel Butler. It consists of octosyllabic couplets, with occasional feminine endings,
of a sharply derisive character, as exemplified in this excerpt
from the poem:

> For his religion it was fit
> To match his learning and his wit;
> 'Twas Presbyterian true blue,
> For he was of the stubborn crew
> Of errant Saints, whom all men grant
> To be the true Church Militant; . . .
> That with more care keep holiday
> The wrong, than others the right way;
> Compound for sins they are inclined to
> By damning those they have no mind to.
> Still so perverse and opposite
> As if they worshipped God for spite; . . .

Although quasi-meditative, quasi-didactic, rather than satiric,
and far more sophisticated than Butler's work, W. H. Auden's
"New Year Letter", written in Hudibrastic couplets, has passages that approach the seventeenth-century man's savage wit,
as where the twentieth-century poet speaks of seeing

> Boys trained by factories for leading
> Unusual lives as nurses, feeding
> Helpless machines, girls married off
> To typewriters, old men in love
> With prices they can never get,
> Homes blackmailed by a radio set,
> Children inherited by slums
> And idiots by enormous sums.

hymnal stanza   See common measure.

hypercatalectic   See catalectic.

hypermetrical   See catalectic.

[I]

iamb   A foot of two syllables, the first short or unstressed, the second long or stressed. See also **metre**, page 88.

iambic   See **metre**, page 88.

ictus   The metrical or rhythmical stress on a syllable usually represented ('). See **thesis**.

identical rhyme   See **rhyme**, page 131.

idyl   See **pastoral**.

image   The representation of a particular thing with faithful, evocative detail, as in Donne's simile:

> And like a bunch of ragged carrets stand
> The short swolne fingers of thy gouty hand.

An image need not be metaphorical, nor is it necessarily visual, as the following instance shows:

> . . . Then a damp gust
>   Bringing rain

Imagery may make an appeal to the senses and also be open to symbolic interpretation. The phrase quoted above would have actuality for a blind man who had never heard a poem by Eliot. To anyone familiar with his work, however, and especially with *The Waste Land*, which is the source of the quotation, the apparently simple sensuous image suggests not merely a change of weather but the possibility of a change of heart and the hope of spiritual regeneration.

imagination   The power or process of using all the faculties so as to realize with intensity both what is and what is not perceived, and to do this in a way that integrates and orders everything thus present to the mind so that reality is enhanced thereby. Coleridge distinguished between the Primary Imagination, which he held to be "the prime agent of all human perception", and the Secondary Imagination, which, though operating in the same way as perception, yet "dissolves, diffuses, dissipates, in order to re-create; . . ." He saw fancy as distinct from both, being merely a process of association, while the secondary imagination relates associated images so that each, in enriching the other, enlarges the reader's understanding. See also **fancy; poetry.**

imagism   Poetry that presents its subject with clarity, accuracy, and economy of language, using metaphor or, more rarely, relying on the statement of the sharply perceived concrete detail to give the quality of an emotion or the atmosphere of a scene with greater precision. When this century was in its teens, the term became the battle-cry of the self-styled **imagists.** Along with definiteness and concision, their cardinal principles included the use of appropriate cadences, in Pound's words, "to compose in the sequence of the musical phrase, not in the sequence of the metronome". The following lines, "To Waken an Old Lady", are an example of an imagist poem composed by William Carlos Williams, one of the earliest members of the group and the one who remained most faithful to their principles:

> Old age is
> a flight of small
> cheeping birds
> skimming

> bare trees
> above a snow glaze.
> Gaining and failing
> they are buffeted
> by a dark wind—
> But what?
> On harsh weedstalks
> the flock has rested,
> the snow
> is covered with broken
> seedhusks
> and the wind tempered
> by a shrill
> piping of plenty.

imagist   See **imagism**.

imitation   is that species of translation "where", according
to Dryden, "the translator (if now he has not lost that name)
assumes the liberty, not only to vary from the words and sense,
but to forsake them both as he sees occasion; and taking only
some general hints from the original, to run division on the
groundwork, as he pleases." W. P. Ker notes that "to run division" is "the common old term for executing variations on
a musical theme." Dryden described three modes of translation, calling the first "metaphrase, or turning an author word
by word, and line by line, from one language into another." The
second he termed "paraphrase, or translation with latitude,
where the author is kept in view by the translator, so as never
to be lost, but his words are not so strictly followed as his
sense; and that too is admitted to be amplified, but not altered."
Dr. Johnson defined imitation as "a method of translating
looser than a paraphrase, in which modern examples or illustrations are used for ancient, and domestick for foreign." Else-

where he called it "a kind of middle composition between translation and original design, which pleases when the thoughts are unexpectedly applicable and the parallels lucky." His own rendering of Juvenal's Tenth Satire, "The Vanity of Human Wishes", is a superb instance of this, with its far from Roman opening:

> Let observation with extensive view
> Survey mankind from China to Peru;

and its many fine passages not to be found in Juvenal. Imitation has been practiced by poets from Cowley to Robert Lowell.

imperfect rhyme   See **rhyme,** page 131.

initial rhyme   See **rhyme,** page 131.

In Memoriam stanza   See **stanza,** page 169.

interlaced rhyme   See **rhyme,** page 131.

internal rhyme   See **rhyme,** page 131.

inversion   Reversal of the normal word order. It was formerly regarded as a legitimate means of preserving the structure of a poem. Shelley used it for the sake of the metre in the line "Thus ceased she: and the mountain shepherds came," and for the sake of the rhyme scheme here:

> . . . my spirit's bark is driven,
> Far from the shore, far from the trembling throng
> Whose sails were never to the tempest given . . .

Such usage is now frowned upon, though skilful craftsmen continue to employ the device, chiefly for the sake of emphasis, as Hardy did in this line: "Down comes the winter rain—". To avoid confusion, the meaning of inversion should be limited to

this sense of the term. It is, however, often used as synonymous
with INVERTED STRESS or INVERTED FOOT.

inverted accent   See **substitution.**

inverted foot   See **substitution.**

inverted stress   See **substitution.**

Ionic   A classical foot of four syllables, of which the first two
are long and the last two short (the **greater Ionic**) or the first two
short and the last two long (the **lesser Ionic**). In English verse
stressed syllables are substituted for the long ones and unstressed
for the short. See also **metre,** page 88.

irony   A statement that contradicts the actual attitude of the
speaker or a situation that contrasts what is expected with what
occurs and always having overtones of mockery. Marianne Moore
is ironical when she begins a poem on "Poetry" with the remark,
"I, too, dislike it . . .". In the following lines Eliot presents
the ironic contrast between the transcendentalist's assertion
and the fact that mocks it:

> (The lengthened shadow of a man
> Is history, said Emerson
> Who had not seen the silhouette
> of Sweeney straddled in the sun.)

Irony may be the motivating element in a narrative poem. Thus,
Robert Penn Warren's "Ballad of Billie Potts" tells the story of
the son of a pair of outlaws who returns home after a long
absence and, before he can be recognized, is robbed and mur-
dered by the parents for whom he had planned a joyful surprise.
This ballad is doubly ironical because the sensational story becomes the symbol of a larger situation and is bound up with the
problem of our identity as Americans and the moral significance

of our history. **Romantic irony** is a quality that belongs to poems which mingle self-pity with self-mockery, as in Byron's lines:

> The heart is like the sky, a part of heaven,
>   But changes night and day, too, like the sky;
> Now o'er it clouds and thunder must be driven,
>   And darkness and destruction as on high:
> But when it hath been scorch'd and pierced and riven
>   Its storms expire in water-drops; the eye
> Pours forth at last the heart's blood turn'd to tears,
>   Which makes the English climate of our years.

Tragic irony informs poetry that acknowledges the contradictions of experience. It is fundamental to the poetry of Yeats, which balances apparent incompatibles. He called "that untroubled sympathy" (the adjective is significant) "for men as they are, as apart from all they do and seem, . . . the substance of tragic irony." For him the supreme aim was "an act of faith and reason to make one rejoice in the midst of tragedy". His acknowledgment that it was "an impossible aim" points to that sense of the incongruous which is essential to tragic irony. This is the theme of "Lapis Lazuli", a poem in which he imagines three Chinamen carved in lapis as living sages who stare "on all the tragic scene" while one plays "mournful melodies", a poem that concludes:

> Their eyes mid many wrinkles, their eyes,
> Their ancient, glittering eyes, are gay.

Auden explores tragic irony in a poem on the attitude of the Old Masters toward suffering: their understanding that it takes place "While someone else is eating or opening a window or just walking dully along"; and he recalls Brueghel's painting of the fall of Icarus, where, for the ploughman, who may have "heard the splash, the forsaken cry", it was "not an important failure", the sun went on shining

> As it had to on the white legs disappearing into the green
> Water; and the expensive delicate ship that must have seen
> Something amazing, a boy falling out of the sky,
> Had somewhere to get to and sailed calmly on.

irregular ode   See **ode**, page 107.

isometrical syllable   One which is reckoned as of equal temporal value with the others in a line of verse. **Isosyllabic verse** is composed of lines containing the same number of isometrical syllables, if no account is taken of stress or quantity. Such verse is said to be employed in the *Avesta*, the sacred writings of the ancient Persians. French syllabic verse is theoretically composed of isosyllabic feet, but in practice stress plays a more significant part than in English syllabic verse.

isosyllabic verse   See **isometrical syllable**.

Italian sonnet   See **sonnet**.

[J]

jongleur   See **troubadour**, page 183.

[K]

kenning   A figurative stock phrase used in Norse and Anglo-Saxon poetry, such as "the whale-road" for the sea. It has its equivalent in the stock epithet—"the wine-dark sea", "ox-eyed Hera", and the like—of the Greek epics, with which translation has made us more familiar.

[L]

lay   A lyric or, more commonly, a short narrative poem often in four-stress couplets and meant to be sung. So "The strings were plucked, many a song rehearsed" at the feast celebrating Beowulf's victory over Grendel, and we are told further (in Kevin Crossley-Holland's translation),

> Thus the lay was sung,
> The song of the poet.

Scott's *Lay of the Last Minstrel* imitates such a verse narrative, though intended to be read or recited without music.

leonine rhyme   See **rhyme**, page 131.

level stress   See **accent**, page 7.

light ending   See **feminine ending**.

light rhyme   See **rhyme**, page 131.

light stress (`)   A metrical stress that falls on a word not emphasized in normal speech, as in Wordsworth's line:

> That thére hath pást awáy a glóry from the eárth.

light verse   Designed to entertain and often as formal in structure as it is slight in tenor, it includes parodies, limericks, clerihews, and other humorous pieces. Auden's anthology of light verse includes poetry written for public performance; poetry of which the subject-matter is "the everyday social life of its period or the experiences of the poet as an ordinary human being"; and nonsense verse having "a general appeal", represented by nursery rhymes and the poems of Edward Lear. Even for those with a less generous view of it, light verse is a more inclusive term than **vers de société**, which may turn a compliment or touch off the manners and morals of the day and, marked as it is by grace, elegance, and wit, sometimes verges on serious verse. It is exemplified in George Wither's lyric, the first stanza of which begins with the query:

> Shall I, wasting despair,
> Die because a woman's fair?

and answers:

> If she think not well of me,
> What care I how fair she be.

Nonsense verse differs from other light verse in depending for its charm not upon wit but upon sheer absurdity. When it relies largely on pure sound, like these lines by Lear, it verges on abstract poetry:

> And in twenty years they all came back,
>   In twenty years or more,
> And everyone said, "How tall they've grown!
> For they've been to the Lakes, and the Torrible Zone,
>   And the hills of the Chankley Bore;" . . .

Nonsense verse is sometimes open to serious interpretation, such as Auden's commentary on Lewis Carroll's *The Hunting of the Snark*, which he reads as a poem about "human society moving through time and struggling with its destiny"—a bleak destiny in view of the Baker's encounter:

> In the midst of the word he was trying to say
>   In the midst of his laughter and glee,

He had softly and suddenly vanished away—
For the Snark *was* a Boojum, you see.

limerick   A popular form of humorous verse of three long and
two short lines rhyming *a a b b a*, popularized by Edward Lear,
who discovered the form in this anonymous example:

There was an old man of Tobago
Who lived on rice, gruel, and sago;
Till, much to his bliss,
His physician said this:
To a leg, sir, of mutton you may go.

The illustration is of historical interest but is not typical, since
as often as not limericks are bawdy, as indicated below.

A limerick packs laughs anatomical
Into space that is quite economical.
But the good ones I've seen
So seldom are clean,
And the clean ones so seldom are comical.

linked rhyme   See **rhyme**, page 131.

L.M.   Abbreviation for long measure. See also **common measure.**

logaœdic   In classical prosody the term applies to lines of
verse that combine iambs and anapests or troches and dactyls in
a group of at least two, and at most four, feet. The term has
come to be used of mixed metres generally. This line by Frost is
logaœdic:

A scent / of ripe / ness from o / ver a wall.

logical stress   See **metre**, page 88.

logical structure   See form.

logopoeia   A term used by Ezra Pound to distinguish that kind of poem in which neither the sound of the words nor the images that they convey are as significant as the effect of unexpected usage. The poet whom he repeatedly cites as charging language in this way is Jules Laforgue. Since the Frenchman's influence is prominent in Eliot's early work, that seems to offer examples of logopoeia in English. They occur when words are used playfully, when their effect is ironic or satiric, above all, when a word or a phrase trailing familiar associations is made to proliferate new meanings. This "dance of the intellect among words" defies translation. **Melopoeia** is Pound's term for the kind of poem in which "some musical property" inherent in the words is intrinsic to and indeed governs their meaning. This, too, is untranslateable but, unlike logopoeia, it can be appreciated by a person ignorant of the sense of the words. If music is, in Dryden's phrase, "inarticulate poetry", melopoeia may perhaps be called articulate music. Pound mentions these types of melopoeia: "(1) that made to be sung to a tune; (2) that made to be intoned or sung to a sort of chant; and (3) that made to be spoken; . . ." Each of these objectives requires a distinct "art of joining words". In addition to logopoeia and melopoeia, he employs the term **phanopoeia**; this refers to a third kind of poem: that which addresses itself chiefly to the visual imagination and which depends almost exclusively upon "utter precision of word". It is the one kind of poem that is amenable to translation. According to Pound, logopoeia, melopoeia, and phanopoeia, "plus 'architectonics' or 'the form of the whole' ", comprise the basis of all writing and emphatically of that most highly charged writing which is poetry.

long measure   See common measure.

lyric   A poem composed to be sung or appropriate for singing and expressive of the personal feeling of the one voicing
it. The following is by Jonson:

> Slow, slow, fresh fount, keep time with my salt teares;
>   Yet slower, yet ô faintly gentle springs:
> List to the heavy part the musique beares,
>   "Woe weepes out her division, when shee sings.
>   Droupe hearbs, and flowres;
>   Fall griefe in showres;
>   Our beauties are not ours":
>   O, I could still
> (Like melting snow upon some craggie hill,)
>   drop, drop, drop, drop,
> Since natures pride is, now, a wither'd daffodill.

A later and simpler example is this by Robert Burns:

> Oh my luve is like a red, red rose,
>   That's newly sprung in June:
> Oh my luve is like the melodie,
>   That's sweetly play'd in tune.
>
> As fair art thou, my bonie lass,
>   So deep in luve am I;
> And I will luve thee still, my dear,
>   Till a' the seas gang dry.
>
> Till a' the seas gang dry, my dear,
>   And the rocks melt wi' the sun;
> And I will luve thee still, my dear,
>   While the sands o' life shall run.
>
> And fare thee weel, my only luve!
>   And fare thee weel a while!

> And I will come again, my luve,
> Tho' it were ten thousand mile!

The contemporary lyric by Léonie Adams quoted below gains in pathos because this "Lullaby" is addressed to an aged man.

> Hush, lullay.
> Your treasures all
> Encrust with rust,
> Your trinket pleasures fall
> To dust.
>
> Beneath the sapphire arch,
> Upon the grassy floor,
> Is nothing more
> To hold,
> And play is over-old.
> Your eyes
> In sleepy fever gleam,
> Their lids droop
> To their dream.
> You wander late alone,
> The flesh frets on the bone,
> Your love fails in your breast;
> Here is the pillow.
> Rest.

Lyric is interchangeable with lyrical as a term of description for poetry of this nature.

[M]

macaronic verse produces a burlesque effect by mixing the vernacular of one or more languages with Latin, and adding Latin terminations to the vernacular words. The term is also used of verse in which any two or more languages are incongruously mingled. An example is found in these lines by Skelton:

> Parrot saves habler Castiliano,
>> With fidasso di cosso in Turkey and in Thrace;
> Vis consilii expers, as teacheth me Horace,
> Mole ruit sua, whose dictates are pregnant,
> Soventez foys, Parrot, en souvenante.

macron See **mora.**

madrigal Originally music, for several voices, composed for a given stanza or a lyric, the word has come to mean a short poem, usually a love lyric, which can readily be set to music. A madrigal, in the sense of a musical setting, has occasionally been composed for a poem that had been written to a different melody. In his pastoral, "Rosalynd", Thomas Lodge entitles a lyric printed for singing, "Rosalynd's Madrigal":

> Love in my bosom like a bee
> Doth suck his sweet;
> Now with his wings he plays with me,
> Now with his feet.
> Within mine eyes he makes his nest,

> His bed amidst my tender breast;
> My kisses are his daily feast,
> And yet he robs me of my rest;
> Ah, wanton, will ye?

masculine ending   See **feminine ending.**

masculine rhyme   See **rhyme**, page 131.

measure   Though sometimes used as synonymous with metre or rhythm, the term commonly means foot. In certain circumstances the Greeks regarded a measure as composed of two feet, and so a **dipody.** Thus in classical Greek verse, an anapestic dimeter is a line of four anapestic feet or two dipodies, an iambic trimeter is a line of six iambic feet or three dipodies, a trochaic tetrameter a line of eight trochaic feet or four dipodies. See also **metre.**

melapoeia   See **logopoeia.**

metaphor   Language that implies a relationship, of which similarity is a significant feature, between two things and so changes our apprehension of either or both. Aristotle said that for the poet "the greatest thing by far is to have a command of metaphor. This alone cannot be imparted by another; it is the mark of genius, for to make good metaphors implies an eye for resemblances." After upwards of two thousand years his view is firmly held. Twentieth-century critics have shown that the making of good metaphors implies an eye for differences, too, and that the meaning of a metaphor issues from more complex interactions of perceptions, feelings, and thoughts than were dreamt of in the good Greek's philosophy. Philip Wheelwright holds metaphor to be "a medium of fuller, riper knowing". That command of metaphor and of its interpretation can help us to conduct our lives well is the claim of I. A. Richards.

We owe to him the terms currently used for the two elements that together constitute a metaphor. The vehicle is the figure that carries the weight of the comparison. The subject to which it refers is called the tenor. Some of the ways in which they collaborate may be seen by examining Yeats's lines on the old man who is but

> A tattered coat upon a stick, unless
> Soul clap its hands and sing, and louder sing
> For every tatter in its mortal dress, . .

The aged man is the tenor, his "soul . . . in its mortal dress" is the vehicle. There are subordinate metaphors here. The body is the tenor of which the "tattered coat upon a stick" and the "mortal dress" are the vehicles. The body is flesh and bone, so that the "tattered coat" is the vehicle of the flesh and "stick" the vehicle of the skeleton. A more detailed study of these lines would show the contributory meanings that emerge from the right use of "the greatest thing by far".

When the vehicle of one metaphor becomes the tenor of another intimately related to it, the result is a **telescoped** or **complex metaphor.** An instance may be taken from *Antony and Cleopatra,* where Caesar says to Antony:

> Let not the peece of Vertue which is set
> Betwixt us, as the Cyment of our love
> To keep it builded, be the Ramme to batter
> The Fortune of it . . .

The woman who is Caesar's sister and Antony's wife is the tenor of which "the peece of Vertue" set betwixt them is the vehicle. The cement of their love that may become the ram to batter its fortune down is the vehicle of that "peace of Vertue". A **subdued metaphor** is one that is merely implied. In these lines love as a structure, whether palace or fortress, that can be built or destroyed by human effort, is such a metaphor.

The unskilful versifier indulges in metaphors that are merely decorative or illustrative, as in a sonnet to Duty which represents that moral excellence as, among other things, a light, a shield, a balm, a comrade, a tonic, a nurse, a mart, a gardener, a spell, and a tyrant. A good metaphor contributes to the presentation and is therefore **functional**. This term is used, synonymously with **structural** and **organic metaphor**, to mean one that relies upon the vehicle to carry an implicit tenor, and in which the vehicle takes on symbolic meaning. Such organic metaphors dominate Shakespeare's plays and are also evident in metaphysical poetry. These stanzas from Donne's "Hymne to God my God, in my Sicknesse" offer an illustration:

> Whilst my Physitians by their love are growne
> Cosmographers, and I their Mapp, who lie
> Flat on this bed, that by them may be showne
> That this is my South-west discoverie
> *Per fretum febris*, by these streights to die,
> I joy, that in these straits, I see my West;
>   For, though theire currants yeeld returne to none,
> What shall my West hurt me? As West and East
> In all flatt Maps (and I am one) are one,
> So death doth touch the Resurrection.

The poet's corruptible body—which "must put on incorruption" as East meets West on a map "in a moment, in the twinkling of an eye . . ."—is the implied tenor. The elaborate vehicle unites physiological and cosmographical imagery here in an organic metaphor that takes on religious symbolism.

Ordinary speech is full of words and phrases no longer recognized as metaphorical, such as "nightfall" or "at break of day", and that are therefore **dead metaphors**. These lines by

Wordsworth offer examples in the verb "flew" and the adjective "idle":

> So through the darkness and the cold we flew,
> And not a voice was idle . . .

A **mixed metaphor** is one in which the suggested resemblance of the things compared is in some respect so false as to be canceled out. Shakespeare's phrase, "to take arms against a sea of troubles", is often mistaken for an example of this; on the contrary, it is a valid metaphor. It refers to the custom attributed to Celtic warriors of fighting the waves with swords drawn; it also suggests that Hamlet's troubles, as threatening as the sea and many like its waves, will not be dismissed thus and returns again to the previous metaphor about suffering "the slings and arrows of outrageous fortune". The highly compressed language of much metaphysical and symbolist poetry results in what seem to be mixed metaphors but may better be called telescoped ones. Thus the opening phrase in Hart Crane's lines

> The calyx of death's bounty giving back
> A scattered chapter, livid hieroglyph

refers, as the poet explained, "in a double ironic sense both to a cornucopia and the vortex made by a sinking vessel. As soon as the water has closed over a ship this whirlpool sends up broken spars, wreckage, etc. which can be alluded to as livid *hieroglyphs* making a *scattered* chapter so far as any complete record of the ship and her crew is concerned".

A **simile** differs from a metaphor in that the tenor and vehicle are identified as such and the fact of their resemblance is clearly indicated by "like" or "as". So Spenser, describing the beauty of the bride, speaks of

> Her cheekes lyke apples which the sun hath rudded,

Her lips lyke cherryes charming men to byte,
Her breast lyke to a bowl of creame uncrudded . . .

Simile is more explicit than metaphor and therefore less evocative. Recognizing this, Philip Wheelwright finds that the distinction between the two kinds of comparison is not merely a grammatical one, depending on the use of "like" or "as"; they differ
in significance. In his view, a simile merely joins two separate
images or ideas, while a metaphor is more complex and inclusive.
From the "fresh relationship" that a metaphor creates between
two or more images and the ideas associated with them, a new
shade of meaning results. He makes his distinction plainer by
observing that "while a dictionary of similes is possible, a dictionary of metaphors is not."

Allegory, in which the tenor is unexpressed and the vehicle
often elaborate, has been called an extended metaphor. It represents one thing in the guise of another, as an abstraction in the
guise of a concrete image, a moral or religious discourse under
the guise of a narrative about a pilgrimage. The characters in an
allegory are apt to be **personifications,** or abstract vices and vir-
tues represented as persons. This is also called **prosopopeia.** Spenser's *The Faerie Queene* is an allegory in the form of a verse
narrative. The savage, ill-favored tempter in the coat of rusty
iron and gold who declares

"God of the world and worldling I me call,
Great Mammon, greatest god below the sky . . ."

is an allegory or personification of worldly wealth. Contemporary
poets reject allegory because of the oversimplification and didac-
ticism that it risks. The use of personification, however, has been
revived by Auden, notably in his memorial poem on Freud, who
is said to have taught "The unhappy Present" how to deal with
the Past and to approach the Future

> Without a wardrobe of excuses, without
>   A set mask of rectitude or an
>   Embarrassing over-familiar gesture.

When fullest use is made of it, metaphor takes on the character of SYMBOL.

metaphrase   See **imitation**, page 69.

metaphysical poetry   The term may mean that which deals with the essential nature of reality, as in the work of Dante and Milton, but since Dr. Johnson singled out Cowley, Donne, and certain other seventeenth-century men as "metaphysical poets", the adjective has been applied chiefly to their highly intellectu- alized work and to later work that exhibits like features. These include the use of images taken from daily life or from scientific pursuits, not for ornament but to express subtleties of thought and feeling vigorously and accurately; the reliance on paradox to the same end; and a movement of the mind so rapid or complex that it tends to obscure the iron logic of the poem. An example of the type is Marvell's "The Definition of Love", which con- cludes:

> As Lines so Loves *oblique* may well
> Themselves in every Angle greet;
> But ours so truly *Paralel*,
> Though infinite can never meet.
>
> Therefore the Love which us doth bind,
> But Fate so enviously debarrs,
> Is the Conjunction of the Mind,
> And Opposition of the Stars.

meter   See **metre**.

metonymy   The substitution of a word that relates to the thing or person to be named for the name itself. Shakespeare makes such a substitution for "sovereign" when he writes, "The crown will find an heir . . .". The term metonymy is sometimes used to include the similar rhetorical device of **synecdoche**: the naming of a part to mean the whole, as in Cowper's lines,

> Toll for the brave!
> The brave that are no more,
> All sunk beneath the wave . . .

where the wave stands for the sea.

metre   The abstract pattern that obtains when rhythm is formally organized. It imposes on verse a regular recurrence of durations, stresses, or syllables that is intended to parcel a line into equal divisions of time. Each of the temporal periods into which the line is divided is called a **foot**. The notion that speech can be fitted to strictly equal periods is now recognized as untenable. Nevertheless, metrical schemes do have a marked regularity. The satisfactions, the happy surprises, of formal versification lie in the relationship between such an abstract temporal scheme and the rhythms of natural speech.

Early in the history of English verse Chaucer lamented the difficulties of being read aright, addressing his "litel book" with the prayer that none "thee mismetre for defaute of tonge". Diversity of opinion as to the correct reading of a given line persists among prosodists. To a poet a good ear is worth a library of treatises on the laws of his craft. The illustrations that follow exemplify rules of which some accomplished poets have been ignorant, which others have ignored, and which are now apt to be questioned or disregarded. The illustrations themselves cannot satisfy every reader, since a poem is open to more varied readings than an orchestral score.

Metres have been based on diverse principles in different regions and in different ages and, of course, have been largely governed by the character of the language. Poets writing in English have used, adapted, or made shift to combine the metrical systems of the Anglo-Saxons, the ancient Greeks and Romans, and the French.

ANGLO-SAXON PROSODY organizes verse on the principles of stress, or intensity of emphasis, and ALLITERATION. The emphasis required by the metre is the **metrical stress** ('). In Anglo-Saxon prosody, as in similar prosodic systems, metrical stress is apt to be reinforced by the emphasis demanded by the meaning. This is usually called the **logical** or **rhetorical stress;** a simpler name for it is **sense stress.** A line from Pound's version of an Anglo-Saxon poem, "The Seafarer", gives the character of this prosody:

> Wáneth the wátch, || but the wórld hóldeth.

Stress prosody governs verse in which the feet are counted by the numbers of stresses to a line. Stress is the notable feature of SKELTONIC or TUMBLING VERSE. In *The Lay of the Last Minstrel* Scott employed stress prosody, as did Coleridge in *Christabel*, the metre of which was founded on the principle of counting in each line the stresses or accents, as he called them, not the syllables. "Though the latter", he said, "may vary from seven to twelve, yet in each line the accents will be found to be only four." Coleridge's arithmetic was not as good as his ear for rhythm, but the principle is well exemplified here:

> There is nót wínd enóugh to twírl
> The one red léaf, the lást of its clán,
> That dánces as óften as dánce it cán,
> Hánging so líght, and hánging so hígh,
> On the tópmost twíg that looks úp at the ský.

Since ACCENT is another word for stress, such verse is also called accentual verse. It is the basis of SPRUNG RHYTHM.

The ancient Greeks and Romans used a metrical system that differs radically from stress prosody. In **classical prosody** emphasis is subordinate to duration. Because such verse depends upon the quantity of time required to utter a syllable, it is called **quantitative verse.** In the classical foot a long syllable occupies twice the time of a short one. Experiments have shown that a stressed syllable tends to be lengthened and a long syllable tends to be stressed. Yet stress and quantity differ as the force of a hammer stroke differs from the duration of the sound it makes. Experiments with quantitative verse in English have been only moderately successful. They are apt to illustrate Longfellow's description of one of his own efforts as verse in which the English Muse moves like "a prisoner dancing to the music of his chains". Among the exceptions some prosodists would include Kingsley's "Andromeda", composed in a close approximation to classical hexameters:

Hovering / over the / water he / came, || upon / glittering /
    pinions,
Living, a / wonder, out / grown || from the / tight-laced / fold
    of his / sandals; . . .

Other examples of quantitative verse in English are given under the names of specific metres: ALCAICS, CHORIAMBICS, ELEGIACS, HENDECASYLLABICS, SAPPHICS.

The determining feature of **syllabic verse** is neither stress nor quantity but the number of syllables in a line. This practice is acceptable for poets writing in a language such as French, where word accent is negligible. The poet using a heavily stressed language such as English may be betrayed into awkwardness. The masters could count their syllables and yet produce admirable cadences, as in these strictly ten-syllable lines by Milton and Pope, respectively:

> A Wildernesse of sweets; for Nature here
> Wantond as in her prime, and plaid at will
> Her Virgin Fancies, pouring forth more sweet,
> Wilde above rule or art; enormous bliss.

> He lifts his tube, and levels with his eye,
> Straight a short thunder breaks the frozen sky:
> Oft, as in airy rings they skim the heath,
> The clam'rous lapwings feel the leaden death:
> Oft, as the mounting larks their notes prepare,
> They fall, and leave their little lives in air.

Among twentieth-century poets, the one notable for writing syllabic verse is Marianne Moore. Indeed, many of her lines, unlike those of her great predecessors, must be counted on the fingers if a metrical pattern is to be perceived in them. Her long poem on the jerboa illustrates her practice. It is composed of stanzas of six lines in which the syllables number 5, 5, 6, 11, 10, 7, as here:

> By fifths and sevenths,
> In leaps of two lengths,
>   like the uneven notes
>   of the Bedouin flute, it stops its gleaning
>   on little wheel-castors, and makes fern-seed
>   foot-prints with kangaroo speed.

These lines by Auden keep to a nine-syllable pattern:

> Blue the sky beyond her humming sail
> As I sit today by our ship's rail
> Watching exuberant porpoises . . .

It is clear that in the lines by Miss Moore and Auden neither stress nor quantity plays a part. Robert Bridges attempted to use an unrhymed "syllabic hexameter" in his *Testament of Beauty*. This twelve-syllable line, based on a carefully elaborated system of ELISION, proved awkward, as a few lines suffice to show. The use of elision in the second and third lines here preserves the proper number of syllables:

> Mortal Prudence, handmaid of divine Providence,
>
> hath inscrutable reckoning with Fate and Fortune:
>
> We sail a changeful sea through halcyon days and storm,
> and when the ship laboureth, our stedfast purpose
> trembles like as the compass in a binnacle.

See also **haiku, tanka, cinquain** for types of syllabic verse. For experiments with Welsh syllabic metres in English verse, see **Welsh forms**, page 190.

Accentual-syllabic verse, commonly used in English poetry, re-places the long and short syllables that compose a line of quan-titative verse with stressed and unstressed syllables; the skilful use of SUBSTITUTION makes for variety, whether it be the substi-tution of one type of foot for another, or of a falling for a rising metre throughout a line. This occurs in what is perhaps the most affecting, as it is certainly the simplest line in English poetry, where Lear recognizes that Cordelia is dead:

> Why should a dog, a horse, a rat have life,
> And thou no breath at all? Thou'lt come no more,
> Never, never, never, never, never.

Although stress rather than quantity is the notable feature of our speech, the terminology of classical prosody is used to describe the metrical devices of verse written in English. We have also adopted the PROSODIC SYMBOLS appropriate to classical verse. Some of those frequently used are given under that head-ing. For the reader's convenience, some appear in parentheses next to the defined term in the body of the text. One foot is divided from another by a virgule or by a line similar to the barline in musical notation. Because of the analogy between the bar and the foot the latter is sometimes called a MEASURE.

The feet most frequently used in our verse are these:

IAMB   ⌣ –   ANAPEST ⌣ ⌣ –

TROCHEE – ⌣   DACTYL   – ⌣ ⌣

A foot composed of iambs or trochees, being one which contains two syllables, is **dissyllabic**. A foot composed of anapests or dactyls, being one which contains three syllables, is **trisyllabic**. Other classical feet that occur often enough in our verse to be noted here include the SPONDEE (– –), the PYRRHIC (⌣ ⌣), the AMPHIBRACH (⌣ – ⌣), the CRETIC (– ⌣ –), the TRIBRACH (⌣ ⌣ ⌣).

The metre of verse composed exclusively or predominantly of iambs, trochees, anapests, dactyls, or spondees is said to be, respectively, **iambic, trochaic, anapestic, dactylic** or **spondaic**. They are illustrated below in lines by Emily Dickinson, W. H. Auden, Tennyson, Dryden, and Milton:

IAMBIC: ⌣ –
     The brain is wider than the sky.
TROCHAIC: – ⌣
     Earth, receive an honoured guest;
     William Yeats is laid to rest:
     Let the Irish vessel lie
     Emptied of its poetry.
ANAPESTIC: ⌣ ⌣ –
     And the peak of the mountain was apples, the hugest that
          ever were seen,
     And they prest, as they grew, on each other, with hardly a
          leaf in between.

DACTYLIC: _ ⌣ ⌣

>   After the pangs of a desperate lover,
>   When day and night I have sighed all in vain,
>   Ah what a pleasure it is to discover
>   In her eyes pity, who causes my pain.

SPONDAIC: _ _

>   . . . these delicacies
>   I mean of Taste, Sight, Smell, Herbs, Fruits, and
>   Flours, . . .

Metrical verse is appropriately described by the number of measures in a line. Here the terminology of classical prosody does not always apply to our verse. The examples of various metres below will illustrate English usage.

Herrick's iambics, "Upon His Departure Hence", offer a rare instance of a lyric in **monometer**, a line composed of a single foot:

>   Thus I
>   Passe by
>   And die:
>   As One,
>   Unknown,
>   And gon :
>   I'm made
>   A shade,
>   And laid
>   I'th'grave:
>   There have
>   My Cave.
>   Where tell
>   I dwell,
>   *Farewell.*

Our **dimeter** is exemplified in this pert stanza from Hardy's poem "The Robin" with its two feet to the line:

When I / descend
Towards / their brink
I stand, / and look,
And stoop, / and drink,
And bathe / my wings,
And chink / and prink.

The **trimeter**, a line of three feet, is illustrated by this stanza
from Lionel Johnson's lyric on the statue of King Charles:

Alone / he rides, / alone,
The fair / and fa / tal king:
Dark night / is all / his own,
That strange / and sol / emn thing.

The **tetrameter** is a line of four feet. It is almost always
broken, as is every longer line, by a pause, not counted in the
timing, called the cesura (||). The monotonous effect of the
tetrameter when it is too regular is satirized in Chaucer's tale

Al of / a knyght || was fair / and gent
In ba / taille and || in tour / nament,

whose name was Sir Thopas.

The **pentameter** is a five-foot line. Introduced by Chaucer,
it has become the commonest of metres, as the iambic is the
commonest type of foot in English verse. "To break the pentameter, that was the first heave!" cried Pound, exercised to lib-
erate our verse from the dead hold of custom. It is, however, one
of the most flexible metres, which helps to account for its dur-
ability. It has been used for such different kinds of poetry as
Chaucer's narratives in verse; Spenser's *The Faerie Queene*; the
blank verse of Elizabethan drama, of Milton's *Paradise Lost*,
and of Wordsworth's *The Prelude*; Dryden's neat couplets; the
irregularly rhymed cantos of Hart Crane's *The Bridge*; Yeats's
lyric "Among School Children"; Wallace Stevens' "Credences

of Summer"; Dylan Thomas's sonnet sequence, "Altarwise by owl-light"; all normal sonnets and many irregular ones; and Karl Shapiro's *Essay on Rime*. What variety is afforded by a line of five stresses with a variable cesura is illustrated in the following examples from Spenser, Milton, Dryden, Wordsworth, Crane, Yeats, Stevens, Thomas, and Shapiro, respectively.

Of mortall life the leaf, the bud, the flowre,

Ore bog or steep, through strait, rough, dense, or rare,

Great wits are sure to Madness near alli'd;
And thin Partitions do their Bounds divide;

The leafless trees and every icy crag
Tinkled like iron, while far distant hills
Into the tumult sent an alien sound
Of melancholy not unnoticed, while the stars
Eastward were sparkling clear, and in the west
The orange sky of evening died away.

Whispers antiphonal in azure swing.

O body swayed to music, O brightening glance,
How can we know the dancer from the dance?

The personae of summer play the characters
Of an inhuman author, who meditates
With the gold bugs, in blue meadows, late at night.

Altarwise by owl-light in the half-way house
The gentleman lay graveward with his furies;

The metric of this book is made upon
The classic English decasyllable
Adapted to the cadence of prose speech;
Ten units to the verse by count of eye

Is the ground rhythm, over which is set
The rough flux and reflux of conversation.

The **hexameter** is a six-foot line, but is so closely associated with classical verse that the term is usually taken to mean the particular form of the line used in antiquity and is illustrated above in the passage on quantitative verse. The English hexameter is exemplified in Longfellow's familiar line:

This is the / forest pri / meval. The / murmuring / pines and
    the / hemlocks . . .

Another six-foot line more natural in English because it is iambic is the ALEXANDRINE.

The seven-foot line or **heptameter** is illustrated in these lines by Hardy:

"O Time, / whence comes / the Moth / er's mood / y look /
    among / her labours,
As of one / who all / unwit / tingly / has wound / ed where /
    she loves?"

The seven-foot line is commonly called the **septenary** after the Latin verse on which it was modeled. The septenary is also known as the **fourteener,** when, as was usual in its flourishing days, it was composed of fourteen syllables. An instance is Golding's version of Ovid's *Metamorphoses:*

More cheerful than the winter's sun or summer's shadow cold,
More seemly and more comely than the plane-tree to behold,
Of value more than apples be although they were of gold . . .

The tiresomeness of much conventional verse is due to devices that force the spoken words to conform closely to the metre. Young Keats, in rebellion against the conformity of Dryden and Pope, exclaimed against them in lines themselves metrically correct:

> Why were ye not awake? But ye were dead
> To things ye knew not of,—were closely wed
> To musty laws lined out with wretched rule
> And compass vile: so that ye taught a school
> Of dolts to smooth, inlay, and clip, and fit,
> Till, like the certain wands of Jacob's wit,
> Their verses tallied.

Even pedantic prosodists of the older school allowed certain departures from the demands of the metre. In iambic pentameter, for example, an unstressed syllable at the close of a line did not make the last foot count as an amphibrach but was accepted as a feminine ending; a trochee might be substituted for an iamb anywhere in the line save in the final foot; and two unstressed syllables might replace one, if elision, actual or theoretical, were possible, as in the third line below:

> Admiration seis'd
> All Heav'n, what this might mean, and whither tend
> Wondring; but soon th' Almighty thus reply'd: . . .

To these procedures, carefully elucidated by Bridges in his study of Milton's prosody, another has been added by J. C. Ransom: "Any two successive iambic feet might be replaced by a double or ionic foot." He uses as an example Donne's line:

> Sŏ, īf / Ĭ drēame / Ĭ hāve / yŏu, Ĭ hāve yōu.

Among the variations that enliven the strict metrical line are ANACRUSIS, CATALEXIS, DISTRIBUTED STRESS, the admission of an EXTRA-METRICAL SYLLABLE, the various forms of COMPENSATION and SUBSTITUTION.

Physical experiments indicate that the ear is satisfied by an approximate temporal equality of the feet in a line. Nevertheless, it is possible to represent the line as conforming more or less to a metrical scheme that presupposes equality. As noted before, one of the pleasures peculiar to strictly metrical verse is the contrast between the pattern of the metre and the speech rhythms. Hopkins spoke of the two as counterpointed. The usual term for the concurrence of two different temporal patterns is **syncopation**. It is evident where the speech rhythm of a line requires a different number of stresses from that required by the metrical scheme. Thus, this line of Milton's has the ten syllables of regular blank verse, which is iambic in character and normally has five stresses, yet it is natural to read the line with only four stresses:

Of púritie and pláce and ínnocénce . . .

The musical effects of Marvell's lyric, "The Garden", are in part due to syncopation. The duple rhythm established at the start,

How váinly mén themsélves amáze

is occasionally counterpointed against a triple rhythm, as in the second line of this couplet:

Annihilating all that's made
To a green / Thought / in a green / Shade.

A similar effect is obvious in these lines by Yeats:

A levelling, rancorous, rational sort of mind
That never looked out of the eye of a saint
Or out of drunkard's eye.

The word accent and the sense stress in the first two lines are counterpointed against the normal iambic beat observable in the third half-line, with resulting syncopation. In larger units, such as a stanza, a long passage from a poem, or a complete lyric, the metre is counterpointed against the rhythm of the spoken phrases. Experiments have shown that readers tend to make

longer pauses than usual in the following passage from Milton
at the points indicated by two virgules; the phrases thus set off
are counterpointed against the iambic decasyllabic metre:

> They ferry over this *Lethean* Sound
> Both to and fro, // thir sorrow to augment, //
> And wish and struggle, as they pass, // to reach
> The tempting stream, // with one small drop to loose
> In sweet forgetfulness all pain and woe, //
> All in one moment // and so neer the brink; //

Coleridge rightly declared that "for any poetic purpose, metre
resembles (if the patness of the simile may excuse the meanness)
yeast, worthless or disagreeable by itself, but giving vivacity and
spirit to the liquor with which it is proportionally combined."
Syncopation may well be the activating enzyme in the liquor
that Milton brewed.

Language, as poets know, is as complex, elastic, and flexible
as any other living thing. The nature of the poet's language, the
character of the artificial pattern to which he makes it more or
less conform, the degree of conformity that he finds desirable, all
contribute to the total effect. That verse moves between speech
and song has become a truism. But if music can be timed with
more accuracy than verse, a temporal pattern can be found in
all but the most pedestrian prose. The growth of more discrimi-
nating studies, complemented by recent work in linguistics, is
enlarging our view of prosodic strategies. Arnold Stein, for one,
has shown how the conflicts between speech rhythms and formal
metrics animate the meanings in a line of verse. The exploration
of metre has only begun.

metrical pause   The so-called metrical pause that occurs at
the end of a line or of a stanza is a misnomer, because, like the
cesura, it has no temporal value in scansion. See **compensation**.

metrical stress   See **metre**, page 88.

Miltonic sonnet   See **sonnet**, page 161.

minnesinger   See **troubadour**, page 183.

mixed metaphor   See **metaphor**, page 82.

Monk's Tale stanza   See **stanza**, page 169.

monometer   A one-foot line. See also **metre**, page 88.

mora   The time, equal to an eighth note in music, occupied by a short syllable in quantitative verse. It is symbolized thus: ⌣. The name of this symbol is a **breve**. The time, which is equal to a quarter note, occupied by a long syllable in quantitative verse is two morae. It is symbolized thus: –. The name of this symbol is a **macron**.

muse   Of the nine goddesses, daughters of Zeus and Mnemosyne, who in Greek mythology presided over the arts and sciences, four held sway over poetry. These were Calliope, Euterpe, Erato, and Polyhymnia, the muses of epic, of lyric, of love, and of sacred poetry, respectively. The Muse is also the particular genius inspiring a poet, so that Milton, meditating on the theme of *Paradise Lost*, cried, "Sing Heav'nly Muse", deliberately invoking her aid for his

> adventrous song,
> That with no middle flight intends to soar
> Above th'*Aonion* Mount, while it pursues
> Things unattempted yet in Prose or Rhime.

Even Shakespeare, to whom the goddess was supremely gracious, exclaimed:

> O! for a Muse of fire, that would ascend
> The brightest heaven of invention, . . .

Earlier, Sidney, biting his tongue and pen, helpless to show his love, was more straightforward: "Fool! said my muse to me, look in thy heart and write." It remained for a twentieth-century poet, Wallace Stevens, to find new forms of address for her whom he calls "the one of fictive music". In one of his essays he conceives her as half-monster yet superhuman, invoking her as "Inexplicable sister of the Minotaur". Robert Graves exalts her as the resplendent, dread White Goddess. More recently Louis MacNeice reminded us that

> Minx or mother, old witch, young coquette,
> And often as not a nun, the Muse will never
> Conform to type . . .

mythopoesis Myth-making, which cannot be entirely relegated to times beyond our knowledge. Blake was a MYTHOPOET, as was Yeats in our own day. In the Proem to *The Bridge* Hart Crane, who shared the need for a cosmology felt by these poets, thus apostrophized the Brooklyn Bridge that was his symbol for power and wisdom:

> O Sleepless as the river under thee,
> Vaulting the sea, the prairies' dreaming sod,
> Unto us lowliest sometime sweep, descend
> And of the curveship lend a myth to God.

The lack of an acceptable or widely accredited myth, that imaginative ordering of experience which helps the group or the person giving it assent to enjoy or endure life and to accept death, is the subject of many contemporary poems.

mythopoet   See **mythopoesis**.

[N]

near rhyme   See **rhyme**, page 131.

neo-classical   See **classical**.

neologism   A new word or phrase, and also a new usage that changes the sense of a word. The inventions of poets have often sprung from a delight in purely aural values. To this group belong the names of the weirdly absurd creatures for whom Edward Lear was responsible: the Yonghy-Bonghy-Bo, the Fimble Fowl, the Bisky Bat, the Pobble who had no toes, the "Dong with the luminous nose". Wallace Stevens, an inveterate neologizer, not only coined words, happily mixing the foreign with the native, but also gave a novel sense to those in the dictionary. Thus, in "Floral Decorations for Bananas" he writes of "pettifogging buds", twisting a word from the law books to describe the rococo décor that he wants "For women of primrose and purl". Frequently a neologism is a matter of onomatopoeia, as where Stevens evokes "thunder's rattapallax". He may, on the contrary, want to stress the prose sense of his invention. So, as he told his Italian translator, he made up the name Oxidia, suggestive of oxidation, for "the typical industrial suburb, stained and grim." Again, the poet will telescope meanings in one word, as Hopkins does in "Spring and Fall", where he writes: ". . . worlds of wanwood leafmeal lie." "Wanwood" combines the sense of "colorless" with the older meaning of wan, which was "dark". W. H. Gardner finds in the sorrowful context a suggestion of wormwood as well. "Leafmeal" suggests the fallen leaves that lie piecemeal, and also the mealy look and texture of fragmented pieces on the ground. *Finnegans Wake* is a prose poem largely composed of such neologisms.

nonsense verse   See **light verse**.

numbers   The term may mean either metrical feet, the metrical line, or verse. When Daniel wrote that "everie Grammarian in this land hath learned his *Prosodia,* and alreadie knowes all this Arte of numbers . . .", he was speaking of the various kinds of feet. When Milton observed that "the true musical delight" of verse "consists only in apt Numbers, fit quantity of Syllables, and the sense variously drawn out from one verse into another", he apparently meant apt or suitable metrical periods, as also when he wrote:

> Then feed on thoughts, that voluntarie move
> Harmonious numbers; . . .

Pope, declaring that he "lisp'd in numbers, for the numbers came", seems to have used the term to mean the metrical line. Elsewhere he wrote scornfully that

> . . . most by Numbers judge a Poet's song:
> And smooth or rough, with them is right or wrong: . . .

Since he went on to say, "These equal syllables alone require . . .", it is evident that here numbers refers to the ten syllables of the conventional line of neo-classical verse.

nursery rhyme   Jingles for children that range from nonsense verse to a couplet by Blake which appeared in an edition of *Mother Goose*:

> A robin redbreast in a cage
> Sets all heaven in a rage.

[O]

objective correlative   A phrase coined by Eliot to signify the concretely realized thing or the situation that objectifies, symbolizes, and re-creates the emotion that the poet wishes to evoke but is not identical with the thing or situation that inspired the poem. Among the objective correlatives in Eliot's work are those sordid tawdry scenes from urban life which present

> such a vision of the street
> As the street hardly understands;

and which, like the dryness of the desert and the dust, "Rock and no water and the sandy road", dismally evoke the failure of our secular civilization. In contrast to these is the garden imagery. It may be as slight as the lilac, the hyacinth, or the rose, but the feeling of release and redemption for which it stands is usually made emphatic by the context, as with the line "But the fountain sprang up and the bird sang down" from "Ash Wednesday". An entire poem, such as "The Love Song of J. Alfred Prufrock", may be an objective correlative, representing in disguised fashion the complex personal feelings out of which it arose.

oblique rhyme   See **rhyme**, page 131.

occasional poetry   That which is composed to commemorate a particular event, casual or significant, sad or festive. The occasional poems of Burns include lines scribbled down on a circus bill, others written on tavern windows, and verses "On the Birth of a Post-humous Child, born in peculiar circumstances of family distress". Among Byron's poems of this type is that written after he swam the Hellespont in imitation of Leander, which ends:

> 'Twere hard to say who fared the best:
> Sad mortals! thus the Gods still plague you!
> He lost his labour, I my jest:
> For he was drowned, and I've the ague.

The occasional poems by Yeats are famous. They include various savage and noble pieces on incidents in recent Irish political and literary history and many personal lyrics. One of these is "Among School Children", which commemorates his senatorial inspection of Irish primary schools and which also speaks feelingly of his concern with the traffic between imagination and reality. The poem opens with the simple statement: "I walk through the long schoolroom questioning:" and closes, after his curse upon old age, with a stanza that is personal yet universally valid, holding an implicit answer to the final question:

> O body swayed to beauty, O brightening glance,
> How can we know the dancer from the dance?

octave   A poem or stanza of eight lines, the term usually referring to the first part of a sonnet. E. A. Robinson wrote a group of twenty-three "Octaves", each a brief meditation in blank verse. He frequently used an eight-line stanza in rhymed trimeters or tetrameters for lyrics and, as here, for dramatic narratives:

> The falling leaf inaugurates
> The reign of her confusion:
> The pounding wave reverberates
> The dirge of her illusion;

And home, where passion lived and died,
Becomes a place where she can hide,
While all the town and harbor side
Vibrate with her seclusion.

The following octave is a complete poem.

What though the moon pours restlessness?
The stars in unison are uttering peace.
The trees are shapes of stillness that no wind,
No birdy shift, rouses from their dark trance.
If there's a soul of stature to address
The night's hugeness, it asks no release.
But one that is ragged, one that is lame and blind,
Shudders to hear the silent heavens dance.

This term is also used when each line of a poem consists of eight
words or syllables.

octosyllabic verse   This consists of eight-syllable lines.

ode   A lyric that is exalted or enthusiastic in tone and,
whether regular or not, elaborately designed. The **regular** form
imitates the triumphal choral odes composed by the Greek poet
Pindar and so is known as the **Pindaric ode.** This consists of a
strophe followed by an antistrophe identical with it in structure and an epode of a different structure. The pattern may be
repeated. STROPHE means a turning, the first part of the Greek
ode having been sung as the chorus moved to one side, the
ANTISTROPHE or counterturn, as it reversed its direction, and the
EPODE or aftersong, also called the STAND, while the chorus stood
still. Jonson's poem to the memory and friendship of Sir Lucius
Carey and Sir Henry Morison is probably the earliest, certainly
one of the finest, examples of the Pindaric ode in English. Turn,
counterturn, and stand are repeated four times, in a pattern
illustrated below by the strophe and epode from the third part.

This last is curious because the poet admitted a broken rhyme to so dignified a composition.

> It is not growing like a tree
> In bulk, doth make man better be;
> Or standing long an oak, three hundred year,
> To fall a log at last, dry, bold, and sear.
> A lily of a day
> Is fairer far, in May,
> Although it fall and die that night;
> It was the plant and flow'r of light.
> In small proportions we just beauties see;
> And in short measures life may perfect be.
>
> Jonson, who sung this of him, ere he went
> Himself to rest,
> Or taste a part of that full joy he meant
> To have expressed
> In this bright asterism;
> Where it were friendship's schism,
> Were not his Lucius long with us to tarry,
> To separate these twi-
> Lights, the Dioscur,
> And keep the one half from his Harry.
> But Fate doth so alternate the design,
> Whilst that in Heav'n, this light on earth must shine.

The **Horatian ode,** named for the Roman poet Horace, is a sequence of formal stanzas such as are found in Keats's "Ode on a Grecian Urn". The English ode is not written for music, among notable exceptions being Dryden's songs composed for St. Cecilia's Day. These are examples of what Cowley miscalled the irregular Pindaric ode. They are not Pindaric, but they are **irregular:** formal in tone but not in structure, the lines and

the stanzas alike varying in length and the rhythm altering with
the tenor. Wordsworth's "Ode on Intimations of Immortality"
is a justly famous instance of the type. The opening strophes
of Tennyson's "Ode on the Death of the Duke of Wellington"
illustrates its character:

> Bury the Great Duke
>   With an empire's lamentation;
> Let us bury the Great Duke
>   To the noise of the mourning of a mighty nation;
> Mourning when their leaders fall,
> Warriors carry the warrior's pall,
> And sorrow darkens hamlet and hall.
>
> Where shall we lay the man whom we deplore?
> Here, in streaming London's central roar,
> Let the sound of those he wrought for,
> And the feet of those he fought for,
> Echo round his bones for evermore.

That the ode seems to be a form alien to the spirit of mid-
twentieth-century poetry is evidenced by Auden's "Ode to Gaea"
in which he speaks of earth as

> . . . our Mother, the
> Nicest daughter of Chaos, . . .

Allen Tate's well-known "Ode to the Confederate Dead" like-
wise carries ironic overtones formerly not usual to poems of this
kind.

off rhyme   See **rhyme,** page 131.

Omar stanza   See **rubaiyat,** page 133.

onomatopoeia   The coining or the use of words that imitate the sound of a thing, as in Tennyson's lines about the farmer's cantering horse:

> Coom oop, proputty, proputty—that's what I 'ears 'im saäy—
> Proputty, proputty, proputty—canter an' canter awaäy.

Onomatopoeia also refers to sound symbolism which does not approximate a precise echo but is strongly suggestive of the thing presented. Linguists bear out the feeling of the unlearned that high tones suggest light and low tones suggest darkness. Jespersen illustrates this with Zangwill's phrase, "The gloom of night, relieved only by the gleam from the streetlamp". Perhaps for reasons connected with the physical act of pronunciation, the short "i" is commonly associated with what is little, the broad "a" with what is large. These and similar considerations affect onomatopoetic verse, which is illustrated below by lines from Shakespeare, Pope, Hopkins, Kipling, and Auden, respectively. See also **verbal texture**.

> . . . and thou, all-shaking thunder
> Smite flat the thick rotundity o' the world!

> Yet let me flap this bug with gilded wings,
> This painted child of dirt, that stinks and stings . . .

> The moon, dwindled and thinned to the fringe ' of a finger-nail
> held to the candle, . . .

> And the fenders grind and heave,
> And the derricks clack and grate, as the tackle hooks the crate,
> And the fall-rope whines through the sheave . . .

> Dear water, clear water, playful in all your streams . . .

open couplet   See **couplet**, page 38.

organic metaphor   See **metaphor**, page 82.

ottava rima   See **stanza**, page 169.

oxymoron   The joining of contradictory terms so as to make an expression more pointed. Thus Henry Vaughn ventures:

> There is in God (some say)
> A deep, but dazling darkness; . . . .

G. M. Hopkins, a poet even when he was writing prose, noted in his Journal that as a pigeon he was watching moved its head, "a crush of satin green came and went, a wet or soft flaming of the light."

[P]

paeon   A foot of four syllables, one long or stressed and three short or unstressed; it is called first, second, third, or fourth paeon according to the position of the long syllable. Hopkins used the first paeon in "The Windhover", as in the phrase about the "dapple-dawn-drawn" falcon.

pantoum   A series of quatrains somewhat similar in structure to the villanelle. Malayan in origin, it was imitated by the French and through their influence has been used, though rarely, by poets writing in English. The second and fourth lines of each quatrain recur as the first and third in the next, and though the number of quatrains is indefinite, the second and fourth lines of the final stanza must repeat the first and third of the first stanza. The anonymous example below shows to what entertaining uses the form lends itself. In order to follow the pattern exactly, the second and fourth lines of the last stanza should be reversed. It is called "Monologue d'outre Tombe" (Monologue from Beyond the Tomb). The Queen referred to at the close is Victoria.

> Morn and noon and night,
>   Here I lie in the ground;
> No faintest glimmer of light,
>   No lightest whisper of sound.
>
> Here I lie in the ground;
>   The worms glide out and in;

No lightest whisper of sound,
    After a lifelong din.

The worms glide out and in;
    They are fruitful and multiply;
After a lifelong din
    I watch them quietly.

They are fruitful and multiply,
    My body dwindles the while;
I watch them quietly;
    I can scarce forbear a smile.

My body dwindles the while,
    I shall soon be a skeleton;
I can scarce forbear a smile,
    They have had such glorious fun.

I shall soon be a skeleton,
    The worms are wriggling away;
They have had such glorious fun,
    They will fertilize my clay.

The worms are wriggling away,
    They are what I have been;
They will fertilize my clay;
    The grass will grow more green.

They are what I have been.
    I shall change, but what of that?
The grass will grow more green,
    The parson's sheep grow fat.

I shall change, but what of that?
    All flesh is grass, one says.
The parson's sheep grow fat,
    The parson grows in grace.

All flesh is grass, one says;
    Grass becomes flesh, one knows.
The parson grows in grace:
    I am the grace he grows.

Grass becomes flesh, one knows.
    He grows like the bull of Bashan.
I am the grace he grows;
    I startle his congregation.

He grows like the bull of Bashan,
    One day he'll be Bishop or Dean.
I startle his congregation;
    One day I shall preach to the Queen.

One day he'll be Bishop or Dean,
    One of those science-haters;
One day I shall preach to the Queen.
    To think of my going in gaiters!

One of those science-haters,
    Blind as a mole or bat;
To think of my going in gaiters,
    And wearing a shovel hat!

Blind as a mole or bat,
    No faintest glimmer of light,
And wearing a shovel hat,
    Morning and noon and night.

parallelism   The repetition of phrases similar in meaning or structure; this device is a feature of Hebrew poetry familiar even to those who know it only in translation. It is illustrated in these lines from Psalm 96:

Let the heavens be glad, and let the earth rejoice;
    let the sea roar, and the fulness thereof;

> let the field exult, and all that is therein:
> Then shall all the trees of the wood sing for joy . . .

Parallelism occurs in the poetry of other Oriental languages, as
also in that of the Finns and of the American Indians. An
instance is a "Navaho Hunting-Song" which begins and ends:

> Comes the deer to my singing,
> Comes the deer to my song,
> Comes the deer to my singing.

It is natural to find it in any incantation and indeed in any
ritual piece, such as the Navaho "Night Chant", with concluding lines that are themselves paralleled elsewhere in the poem:

> In old age wandering on a trail of beauty, lively, may
>   I walk.
> In old age wandering on a trail of beauty, lively again,
>   may I walk.
> It is finished in beauty.
> It is finished in beauty.

The title of Pound's "Night Litany" promises the parallelisms in
which it abounds and which a few lines suffice to show:

> O God, what great kindness
>   have we done in times past
>   and forgotten it,
> That thou givest this wonder unto us,
>   O God of waters?
> O God of the night,
>   What great sorrow
> Cometh unto us,
>   That thou thus repayest us
> Before the time of its coming!

The device is apt to occur in any poem of an exalted or specifically religious nature, as in the following passages by Blake, Whitman, and Eliot, respectively:

> "Tell me what is the night or day to one o'erflowed with woe?
> Tell me what is a thought, & of what substance is it made?
> Tell me what is a joy, & in what gardens do joys grow? . . ."

Smile O voluptuous and cool-breath'd earth!
Earth of the slumbering and liquid trees!
Earth of departed sunset—earth of the mountains misty-topt!
Earth of the vitreous pour of the full moon just tinged with blue!
Earth of shine and dark mottling the tide of the river!

> Where the bricks are fallen
> We will build with new stone
> Where the beams are rotten
> We will build with new timbers
> Where the word is unspoken
> We will build with new speech

paraphone   See **rhyme**, page 131.

paraphrase   See **imitation**, page 69.

pararhyme   See **rhyme**, page 131.

Parnassian poetry   The formal and objective kind of poetry that was composed by the so-called Parnassian school which flourished in France toward the middle of the nineteenth century. The adjective has come to be applied to other verse of that description. Hopkins used the term arbitrarily to signify work by any established poet that is typical of his performance but not at its highest level.

Parnassus   The name of a mountain that in ancient Greece

was sacred to Apollo and the Muses, and so the word has come
to symbolize the arts, especially poetry.

pastoral   A poem about shepherds and other herdsmen or in
praise of such a life as they lead, but often deceptive in its simplicity, since it may be the vehicle of a grave theme unrelated
to the rural scene. The fact that the pastor is the leader of his
human flock can be implied or developed so as to give a pastoral
symbolic significance. Not seldom the pastoral is an elegy, of
which Milton's "Lycidas" is probably the most noteworthy
example in English. W. B. Yeats, writing about one of his
several elegies for Major Robert Gregory, "Shepherd and Goat-
herd", rightly called it "a pastoral" and observed that he had
modeled it on a poem of Vergil's and on Spenser's lament for
Sidney. An **idyl**, another name for the pastoral, means more
specifically a short poem offering a happy picture of country
life. It is associated with Theocritus, whose first idyl begins
with the words of Thyrsis the shepherd:

> The whisper of the wind in
>   that pine-tree,
>   goat-herd,
> is sweet as the murmur of live water;
>   likewise
>   your flute-notes . . .

These lines are from William Carlos Williams' version of the
poem. The Greek poet's idyls furnished a model for Vergil's
Eclogues and both have been widely imitated. The **eclogue,**
also called the **bucolic,** is synonymous with pastoral but usually
refers to a dialogue between two herdsmen. Pastoral and bucolic
are also used as adjectives to describe poetry dealing sympa-
thetically with country themes. The eclogue is apt to carry a
religious or ethical message and more recently to express the

poet's social philosophy. Thus Frost, who gives Vergilian names to the speakers in "Build Soil", ends this "political pastoral" with Tityrus advising Meliboeus to join few gangs if any:

> Join the United States and join the family—
> But not much in between unless a college.

Another contemporary example is Allen Tate's "Eclogue of the Liberal and the Poet", which concludes with the Liberal demanding, "Shepherd, what are we talking about?" and the Poet desperately responding, "Oh, why, Shepherd, are we stalking about?" Louis MacNeice wrote an "Eclogue from Iceland", in which the ghost of Grettir, the Icelandic hero, declares that "Hatred of hatred, assertion of human values" is now the only duty of those he addresses, and when one of the two other speakers asks, "Is it our only duty?" replies:

> Yes, my friends, it is your only duty.
> And, it may be added, it is your only chance.

pathetic fallacy   A phrase coined by Ruskin to characterize the false impression of external things produced by violent emotion. It is found in lines that inappropriately ascribe human feelings to nature, as where Shelley says that

> . . . sunset may breathe, from the lit sea beneath,
> Its ardours of rest and of love . . .

The pathetic fallacy is to be distinguished from empathy, an awareness, more intimate than sympathy, of the feelings of another person and, more narrowly, of the feelings that something not sentient might be supposed to have. Thus Shapiro writes of "A Cut Flower":

> Yesterday I was well, and then the gleam,
> The thing sharper than frost cut me in half.

> I fainted and was lifted high. I feel
> Waist-deep in rain. My face is dry and drawn.

pause   See **compensation**. See also **metrical pause; rhythmical pause.**

pentameter   A five-foot line of verse. **Elegiac pentameter** consists of two dactyls or spondees, a long syllable, two dactyls and a long syllable. See **metre**, page 88. See also **elegiacs.**

perfect rhyme   See **rhyme**, page 131.

personification   See **metaphor**, page 82.

Petrarchan sonnet   See **sonnet.**

phanopoeia   See **logopoeia**, page 78.

phantasy   See **fancy.**

phoneme   One of a class of similar speech sounds that vary in accordance with their phonetic condition, such as environment, quantity, stress, intonation; it is the minimal unit in the sound system of a language, serving to distinguish one utterance from another. Thus, the English phonemes "v" and "w" distinguish "verse" and "worse". So slight is the difference between variants of a phoneme that sometimes only the trained ear can hear it. The sound of "t" in "poetry", "poetic", and "poet", or the sound of "o" in "poem" and in "post" illustrate the difference between variants of the same phoneme. Words that differ semantically, like "bear" and "bare", may be composed of identical phonemes. It is believed that an examination of English in terms of its phonemes would lead to a better understanding of our prosody. In an effort to determine its nature more precisely, it has been studied with machine-age instruments. Tape recordings of poems, one made by Robert Frost among others, of his lyric, "Mowing", have been subjected to minute analysis. Over the years prosodic scholarship has developed a new terminology. These discriminations are made largely by and for those concerned with linguistics, and are not useful to the practitioner. They may eventually become so, especially if the art of poetry is linked more intimately with utterance.

phonemics   is the study of the minimal groups of distinctive speech sounds.

Pindaric ode   See **ode**.

poem   A composition that partakes of the nature of both speech and song, and occasionally relies chiefly on typography. It is nearly always rhythmical, usually metaphorical, and often exhibits such formal elements as metre, rhyme, and stanzaic structure. William Carlos Williams called it "a small (or large) machine made of words", adding that "there can be no part, as in any other machine, that is redundant". Similarly, W. H. Auden remarked that ". . . whatsoever else it may be, a poem is a verbal artifact which must be as skilfully and solidly constructed as a table or a motorcycle". It is chiefly distinguished by the feeling that dictates it and that which it communicates, the economy and resonance of the language, an imaginative power that integrates, intensifies, and enhances experience. These qualities are found only intermittently in prose, and one of the notable features of a poem is that it cannot be paraphrased without injury to its full meaning. See also **poetry**.

poesy   An archaic word for the craft of poetry or for an example of it. Like some other archaisms, the word is accepted as poetic diction. Keats uses "Sleep and Poetry" as the title of a work in which he exclaims:

> O for ten years, that I may overwhelm
> Myself in poesy; so I may do the deed
> That my own soul has to itself decreed.

In our own day William Carlos Williams, delineating the commonplace, writes:

> Out of such drab trash as this
> by a metamorphosis
> bright as wall paper or crayon
> or where the sun casts ray on ray on
> flowers in a dish, you shall weave
> For Poesy a gaudy sleeve . . .

poet   A maker, in its first sense, who works with words. The poet is a person of sensibility who uses words to discover and explore the world, both inner and outer. He finds out the quality of an experience, great or trivial, terrible or gay, by talking, perhaps by singing, to himself. He tries to re-create and so to extend the experience; at the same time he attempts to understand it. The poem is the way in which he makes these efforts, as it is also the result of them. It is the bridge between the world and himself, across which the reader walks for a livelier, a wider, or a deeper view. The term "poet" is sometimes used of those who have the imagination if not the skill peculiar to writers of poetry. As Sidney put it, "One may bee a Poet without versing, and a versifyer without Poetry."

poetaster   An unskilled or trivial versifier.

poetic   Having the qualities associated with the art of poetry and with the capacities of those who practice it. See also **poetic diction; poetic license; poetics.**

poetic diction   Words and phrases not in common use, or an obviously artificial arrangement of them dictated by the belief that the language of poetry should be distinguished from that of prose. This example is by Joseph Warton:

> Her flowing train, and long ambrosial hair,
> Breathing rich odours, I enamour'd view.

The arguments of Wordsworth and Coleridge for and against poetic diction are part of literary history. The subject has been one of the chief themes of twentieth-century poetry. So one finds Eliot demanding

> An easy commerce of the old and the new,
> The common word exact without vulgarity,
> The formal word precise but not pedantic . . .

Wallace Stevens introduced the concept of THE ANTI-POETIC, which he called "that truth, that reality to which all of us are forever fleeing". The flight to reality, to the world given us by our senses and by our experience of life, becomes apparent in the language of the fleeing poet. The need for the anti-poetic recurs. Shakespeare was speaking for himself as well as for his protagonist when he wrote:

> Henceforth my wooing mind shall be express'd
> In russet yeas and honest kersey noes.

Among contemporaries, one of its chief partisans was William Carlos Williams, who observed:

> Things, things unmentionable
> the sink with the waste farina in it and
> lumps of rancid meat, milk-bottle-tops: have
> here a still tranquillity and loveliness
> Have here (in his thoughts)
> a complement tranquil and chaste.

Stevens writes similarly in a passage about dewlike tissues and gems:

> heads
> Of the floweriest flowers dewed with the dewiest dew.
> One grows to hate these things except on the dump.

"Is it peace," he asks,

> Is it the philosopher's honeymoon, one finds
> On the dump?

He continually meditated on the relationship between the anti-poetic fact and the poetic fiction. Harping, almost literally, upon the necessary interplay between reality and imagination, he of course harped as well on the movement between poetic diction and common speech, insisting that

> The poem goes from the poet's gibberish to
> The gibberish of the vulgate and back again.

poetic license   Any departure from the rules of pronunciation or diction, for the sake of rhyme or metre, or an unjustifiable departure from fact. Gascoigne says: "This poeticall license is a shrewde fellow, and covereth many faults in a verse; it maketh wordes longer, shorter, of mo sillables, of fewer, newer, older, truer, falser; and, to conclude, it turkeneth [alters] all things at pleasure . . .". Among the examples he gives are the substitution of "orecome" for "overcome" and "tane" for "taken". Little Marjorie Fleming made fun of her own freedoms in more than one of her bits of verse, as in the lines on the death of James II:

> He was killed by a cannon splinter,
> Quite in the middle of the winter;
> Perhaps it was not at that time,
> But I can get no other rhyme.

Sir John Harrington translates an "old verse" defending poetic license thus: "Astronomers, Painters, and Poets may lye by authoritie." But he cites it only to refute it, claiming that poets "lye least of all other men", since they do not pretend their fictions to be fact, and, moreover, conceal deep truths in the guise of fable.

poetics   Seldom used in the singular, this signifies writing that deals with the art of poetry or presents a theory of the art. The most famous instance of such a treatise is Aristotle's *Poetics*. The word may have the narrower meaning of a study of versification. It also means a poetic composition but is rarely so employed.

poetry   The art which uses words as both speech and song, and, more rarely, as typographical patterns, to reveal the realities that the senses record, the feelings salute, the mind perceives, and the shaping imagination orders. This definition is offered with some diffidence and should be read together with a few by other poets. Sidney said that poetry is "a representing, counterfetting, or figuring foorth: to speak metaphorically, a speaking picture: with this end, to teach and delight". Wordsworth called it "the breath and finer spirit of all knowledge . . . the impassioned expression which is the countenance of all Science".

Coleridge offered several definitions, all worth meditating. Perhaps the most pregnant occurs in that passage in which he writes: "What is poetry? is so nearly the same question with, what is a poet? that the answer to the one is involved in the solution of the other." He describes the poet "in *ideal* perfection" as bringing "the whole soul of man into activity, with the subordination of its faculties to each other, according to their relative worth and dignity". This is the work of the imagination, that power which "reveals itself in the balance or reconciliation of opposite or discordant qualities: of sameness, with difference; of the general, with the concrete; the idea, with the image; the

individual, with the representative; the sense of novelty and
freshness, with old and familiar objects; a more than usual state
of emotion, with more than usual order; judgment ever awake
and steady self-possession, with enthusiasm and feeling pro-
found or vehement; and while it blends and harmonizes the
natural and the artificial, still subordinates art to nature; the
manner to the matter; and our admiration of the poet to our
sympathy with the poetry". This is less open to question than
most of the statements that follow, though each merits a degree
of consideration.

To Shelley the art was "the record of the best and happiest
moments of the happiest and best minds". Arnold held that
"poetry is at bottom a criticism of life . . .". Hopkins defined
it as "speech framed . . . to be heard for its own sake and
interest even over and above its interest of meaning". Stevens
found it to be "a revelation in words by means of the words".
Auden once said that the Devil had fathered it because "poetry
might be defined as the clear expression of mixed feelings."
Dylan Thomas called it "the rhythmic, inevitably narrative,
movement from an overclothed blindness to a naked vision . . . ."

Poetry includes a lyric on a flea bite and *The Divine Comedy*,
along with countless pieces on the horrors of war, the terror of
death, the pleasures of drink and of love. The most solitary
celebration, the loneliest lament, the briefest excitement and
the most penetrating insight into man's estate can be shared
when whatever has aroused feeling, and the feelings themselves,
are ordered and enhanced in a poem. This is the metamorphosis
that humanly redeems the human condition. The distinction
between poetry and verse is at least as old as Sidney, who spoke
of the latter as "but an ornament and no cause to Poetry, sith
there have beene many most excellent Poets that never versified,
and now swarme many versifiers that neede never aunswere to

the name of Poets . . . it is not riming and versing that maketh a Poet, no more than a long gowne maketh an Advocate, who though he pleaded in armor should be an Advocate and no Souldier." For Sidney poetry lay in "delightful images" and "delightful teaching", though he admitted that "the Senate of Poets hath chosen verse as their fittest rayment . . .". Eliot, without defining the difference, implies that verse is a matter of structure, while poetry is marked by intensity of feeling and gravity of import, which find expression in a musicianly concern for resonance in both the sounds and the associations of the words chosen. The distinguishing feature of verse is its formal aspect, that of poetry is its imaginative power.

polyphonic prose   A poem that is set down on the page as prose and is closer to the rhythms of prose than to those of verse. It exhibits such devices as rhyme, assonance, alliteration, and parallelism. An off-shoot of free verse, it was used chiefly by Amy Lowell, the author of the following lines, a fragment of a long piece in this genre:

> In a pattern like a country dance, each balanced justly by its neighbour, lightly, with no apparent labour, the ships slip into place, and lace a design of white sails and yellow yards on the purple, flowing water. Almighty Providence, what a day! Twenty-three ships in one small bay, and away to the Eastward, the water of old Nile rolling sluggishly between its sand-bars.

poulter's measure   The name given to the alternation of the alexandrine and the fourteener popular in the sixteenth century because, as Gascoigne wrote, "it giveth xii for one measure and xiiij for another." Obviously, here measure meant not the foot but the line.

primary accent   See **accent.**

projective verse   A term coined by Charles Olson, who views verse as a projection of energy, declared in a sequence of perceptions that move as in a chain reaction, the form—which is never conventional—being, he affirms, an extension of the content. Intrinsic to such verse, which is sometimes called "composition by field", is the effect of the poet's breathing, on syllable and line, utterance and pause. The typographical arrangements made possible by the typewriter allow the reader to appreciate, as he could not heretofore, what the poet's ear dictates. Olson envisages reliance on "the full relevance of [the] human voice" making for content of larger scope and resulting in the advance of dramatic and epic poetry.

prose poem   Seemingly a contradiction in terms, the phrase may refer to a passage, usually short, of non-discursive prose, the poetic quality of which is self-evident, or to a long work, which, although printed as prose, because of the prominence of the rhythms, the rich connotations of the language, the scope and significance of the whole, can properly be called a poem. Such a work is *Finnegans Wake*, by James Joyce. Pater's tribute to the Mona Lisa is an example of a prose poem of the other kind. Yeats would have quarrelled with this description, perhaps, for while he included the passage in his anthology of modern poetry, he printed the lines as free verse.

prosodic symbols   Signs indicating the long and short, stressed and unstressed syllables that compose the various types of foot, as also other signs used in the scansion of metrical verse. The list below gives the symbols frequently used and the metrical elements that they represent. See also **metre; mora; quantity; rhyme scheme; stanza; thesis.**

‿	short syllable
‿ *or* x	unstressed syllable
–	long syllable
– *or* ´	stressed syllable
⌣ *or* ≍	variable syllable
`	light stress
⌢	distributed stress
o	syllable unmarked by stress or quantity
‖	cesura
∧	rest or hold
/	virgule

prosody   The principles of verse structure. These involve diverse elements, such as the stress, duration, and number of the syllables in a line, the nature and distribution of vowels and consonants, rhythm, metrical scheme, stanzaic pattern, and, of course, the character of the language itself. The feature that appears to govern a system of versification gives its name to that particular prosody.

prosopopeia   See **metaphor**, page 82.

prothalamion   See **epithalamion.**

pure poetry   That which is innocent of any design to instruct, improve, or convert the reader. Such poems, delightful for their melody and their imagery, may be as impersonal as one of Shakespeare's songs, may vibrate with the anguish of Mallarmé, seeking to express the ineffable, or may be luminous with the ·vision that inspired certain songs of Blake. These anonymous lines are pure poetry:

> The maidens came
> When I was in my mothers bower.
> I had all that I wolde.
> The baily berith the bell away,

> The lilly, the rose, the rose I lay,
> The silver is whit, red is the golde,
> The robes they lay in folde,
> The baily berith the bell away,
> The lilly, the rose, the rose I lay;
> And through the glasse window
> Shines the sone.
> How shuld I love and I so young?
> The baily berith the bell away,
> The lilly, the rose, the rose I lay.

The purest poetry is meaningless euphony. It is exemplified in compositions by the French poets who practice what they call *lettrisme*.

pyrrhic   A foot of two short or unstressed syllables. See **metre**, page 88.

[Q]

quantitative verse   See **metre**, page 88. See also **alcaics; choriambics; elegiacs; hendecasyllabics; quantity; sapphics.**

quantity   In Greek and Latin verse the time required to pronounce a syllable. A syllable was counted long if it contained a long vowel or a short vowel followed by two or more consonants. A long syllable counted as equal to two short ones. They are analogous, respectively, to a quarter note and an eighth note in music. Experiments have shown that approximately the same ratio obtains when English verse is read aloud. Nevertheless, the length of a word varies greatly with its position in the line, and its length is affected by a pause. Quantity is an essential, but not a dominant, feature of English verse. See also **metre; prosodic symbols.**

quatrain   A four-line stanza. As strict tetrameter, varied occasionally by substitution, and usually rhymed *a b c d*, it was made fashionable in the first quarter of this century by T. S. Eliot, who employed it for satiric verse, illustrated by these lines from "The Hippopotamus";

> The hippopotamus's day
> Is passed in sleep; at night he hunts;
> God works in a mysterious way—
> The Church can sleep and feed at once.

See also **common measure; rubaiyat.**

[R]

recessive accent   One that falls on the first syllable of a word now normally accented on the second syllable. This line of Shakespeare's provides an instance of recessive accent, "Or I with grief and éxtreme rage shall perish". He sometimes placed the stress on the second syllable of the same word, thus:

> Of one not easily jealous, but, being wrought,
> Perplexed in the extréme . . .

refrain   See **stanza**, page 169.

regular ode   See **ode**.

rest   A pause that counts in the timing. See also **compensation**.

reversed consonance   See **rhyme**, page 131.

reversed foot   See **substitution**.

rhetorical stress   See **metre**, page 88.

rhyme   The repetition of the same or similar sounds, whether vowels, consonants, or a combination of these in one or more syllables, usually stressed and occurring at determined and recognizable intervals. The spelling RIME is close to that of the Old English word, meaning number or reckoning, from which ours comes. That meaning suggests some relation to the temporal periods of verse, and indeed a study of the physical basis of rhyme shows precisely how it functions as an element of rhythm.

The vowels of our language appear to correspond to the steps of the chromatic scale in music. The return to a stressed vowel with its following consonants, as in the **end-rhymes** that conclude lines of conventionally rhymed verse, affords the satisfaction of the return to the keynote in a melody. The tendency to linger on this regularly recurring echo helps to set off the line as a rhythmic entity not unlike a musical phrase, and to organize rhymed stanzas into more elaborate rhythmic patterns.

Internal rhymes, occurring within the line, naturally emphasize rhythmic structure. They are also called **leonine rhymes** after Leo of St. Victor, who used them in his verse. When the syllable before the cesura rhymes with the final syllable, as it did in Leo's elegiacs, the result is to break the long line into two short ones, thus:

"Spanish ships of war at sea! we have sighted fifty-three!"
Then sware Lord Thomas Howard: " 'Fore God I am no coward;
But I cannot meet them here, for my ships are out of gear,
And the half my men are sick. I must fly, but follow quick.
We are six ships of the line; can we fight with fifty-three?"

The final line in this stanza of Tennyson's, like the two first, here omitted, is not broken by leonine rhyme and so relieves what otherwise would be the monotonous rhythm it creates. Internal rhyme need not, of course, occur at the medial pause in the line, and it can assist subtle rhythmic effects. Swinburne used it often, as here:

Who shall say of the wind's way
That he journied yesterday,
Or the track of the storm that shall sound tomorrow,
If the new be more than the grey-grown sorrow?

He also used **interlaced** or **crossed rhyme,** which occurs in a long rhymed couplet so as to break it into four alternating rhyming short lines:

Will ye bridle the deep sea with reins, will ye chasten the high
    sea with rods?
Will ye take her to chain her with chains, who is older than
    all ye Gods?

The effect of consonants has not been so carefully studied as that of vowels, but they seem to have the effect of drumbeats and thus also work to establish rhythm.

Alliteration, sometimes called **head rhyme** or **initial rhyme,** is the echo of the first sound of several words in a line. Repeated initial consonants marked the stressed syllables of Anglo-Saxon verse, while any initial vowel alliterated with any other. It was imitated, supposedly by Langland, in the fourteenth-century poems *Piers Plowman*:

> In a somer seson · Whan soft was the sonne,
> I shope me in shroudes · As I a shepe were,
> In habite as an heremite · Unholy of workes,
> Went wyde in this world · Wonderes to here.

Alliteration has since been widely if less strictly used, as in Donne's lines:

> That I may rise, and stand, o'erthrow mee', and bend
> Your force, to break, blowe, burn and make me new.

Blake used it delightfully here:

> Over the waves she went in wing'd exulting swift
>   delight, . . .

It is found in these lines from Robert Lowell's version of Juvenal's "The Vanity of Human Wishes":

those tombs a twisting fig tree can uproot,
for tombs too have their downfall and their doom.

Langland's contemporary, Chaucer, influenced by French and
Italian verse, was foremost among the English poets who employed rhyme. His very pleasure in it as a source of melody made
him sensitive to its abuse, which he burlesqued in his "Tale of
Sir Thopas" whose "drasty ryming" was declared not worth a
turd. Within a few generations another scholarly craftsman,
Ben Jonson, was railing in "A Fit of Rhyme Against Rhyme":

> He that first invented thee,
> May his joynts tormented bee,
> Cramp'd forever;
> Still may Syllabes jar with time,
> Still may reason warre with rime,
> Resting never.

Milton, who had used it so handsomely in his own lyrics, declared rhyme to be "the Invention of a barbarous Age, to set off
wretched matter and lame Meeter". Dr. Johnson, on the contrary, was convinced of the superiority of rhyme over blank verse,
remarking of a professor of literature whom he disliked, "had
I known that he loved rhyme as much as you tell me he does,
I should have HUGGED him". The device was too useful to
rhythm and too admirable as an ornament to be abandoned.
Yet the man who did not scruple to translate the *Iliad* into
chiming couplets was properly scornful of those who offer the
"sure returns of still expected rhymes", which he proceeded
to illustrate:

> If crystal streams with pleasing murmurs 'creep',
> The reader's threatened (not in vain) with 'sleep' . . .
>
> POPE

By rarely rhyming one noun with another, or one verb with another, he was better able to avoid "expected rhymes". He sometimes used rhyme to point an epigram:

> Man, like the gen'rous vine, supported lives;
> The strength he gains is from th' embrace he gives.

Where there is only one stressed syllable, as here, the rhyme is a masculine one. When the stressed syllable is followed by an unstressed one, the rhyme is feminine, or double, as in Auden's couplet:

> Art in intention is mimesis
> But, realised, the resemblance ceases

Triple rhymes, in which the stressed syllable is followed by two unstressed ones, are unusual, except where the poet is trying for a comic effect, as in these lines from one of W. S. Gilbert's lyrics:

> Though never nurtured in the lap
>   Of luxury, yet I admonish you,
> I am an intellectual chap,
>   And think of things that would astonish you.

That triple rhyme can also serve serious verse is evidenced by more than one poem of Hardy's, such as this:

> When the wasting embers redden the chimney-breast,
> And Life's bare pathway looms like a desert track to me,
> And from hall and parlour the living have gone to their rest,
> My perished people who housed them here come back to me.

Triple rhyme also refers to three rhyming lines such as occur once in rhyme royal and twice in ottava rima.

When lines of verse end in words that are pronounced differently but spelled alike they offer an **eye rhyme**, as in Yeats's lines:

> Many times man lives and dies
> Between his two eternities . . .

If words that are eye rhymes to a later generation were so pronounced in the poet's time as to echo one another truly, they are known as **historical rhymes**. Shakespeare offers good instances of this; witness the opening lines of Sonnet LXII:

> Sinne of selfe-love possesseth al mine eie,
> And all my soule, and al my every part;
> And for this sinne there is no remedie,
> It is so grounded inward in my heart.

Historical rhymes are not always eye rhymes. The former occur, irrespective of spelling, whenever words that were pronounced alike in an earlier period no longer rhyme perfectly to the ears of a later generation. Pope's verse offers instances of historical rhymes such as this:

> Good-nature and good-sense must ever join;
> To err is human, to forgive, divine.

In the examples above, the initial consonants of the words differ, while the stressed vowel and succeeding consonants are the same. These are **full** or **perfect rhymes**. The latter term has also been used for **rime riche**, which occurs when the words are identical in sound, although the sense differs. Rich rhyme is admired in France but seldom used by English-speaking people. Nevertheless, rich rhyme has been admitted into English verse, as where Chaucer rhymes the name of the heroine of *Troilus and Criseyde* with the Middle English spelling of "said", thus:

> Have mercy, swete herte myn, Criseyde!
> And if that, in the wordes that I seyde,
> Be any wrong, I wol no more trespace;

Identical rhyme, the repetition of the same word, is considered a defect, unless the repetition is not the sign of the poet's want of skill but in some way serves his purpose by insistence, as in these lines by Coleridge:

> Then all averred, I had killed the bird
> That brought the fog and mist.
> 'Twas right, said they, such birds to slay,
> That bring the fog and mist.

To relieve the monotony of full rhyme, poets have introduced certain variations of it. Among these is **light rhyme,** where the final rhyming syllable of a word is unstressed. This often occurs in the old ballads and has been deliberately adopted by sophisticated craftsmen. Marianne Moore employs light rhyme often, as when she remarks, à propos of the straitened circumstances of the Sahara field mouse, that

> one would not be he
> who has nothing but plenty.

Miss Moore, like other witty poets from Ben Jonson to Ogden Nash, delights in **broken rhyme.** The term is something of a misnomer, since what is broken is rather the word in order to produce a rhyme. The effect is apt to be comic. Yet such a serious poet as Hopkins took this liberty in order to compel the reading of his verse as he wished it to be read, "with the ears". An example is found in these lines from an untitled sonnet:

> My cries heave, herds-long; huddle in a main, a chief
> Woe, world-sorrow; on an age-old anvil wince and sing—

Then lull, then leave off. Fury had shrieked 'No lingering! Let me be fell: force I must be brief'.

Near rhyme includes the more or less radical substitutes for
full rhyme and its variants. These substitutes have also been
called APPROXIMATE, EMBRYONIC, HALF, IMPERFECT, OBLIQUE, OFF,
and SLANT RHYME, PARAPHONES, and PARARHYMES. As was the
case with light rhyme, some near rhymes occurred in primitive
poetry because the writer was careless or ignorant. Once scorned
by skilful poets, they have come to be approved as ornaments
of verse and as functional devices.

Among the kinds of near rhyme now admired is **assonance,**
where the stressed vowels in the words agree but the consonants
do not. This is also called **vocalic assonance.** A commonplace
in popular balladry, it is found in the second and fourth lines of
this stanza from "Fair Annie":

> 'Bind up, bind up your yellow hair,
> And tie it on your neck;
> And see you look as maiden-like
> As the day that first we met.'

Collins' unrhymed "Ode to Evening" is an example of its melodic uses, as witness his handling of the vowels in the opening
lines:

> If ought of Oaten Stop, or Pastoral Song,
> May hope, O pensive *Eve*, to sooth thine Ear,
> Like thy own brawling Springs,
> Thy Springs, and dying Gales . . .

Originally a rarity in carefully wrought English verse, assonance
was a prominent feature in the poetry of G. M. Hopkins and
more recently in that of Dylan Thomas. Both used it together
with full rhyme so as to achieve maximum resonance. Wilfred

Owen, whose influence on twentieth-century verse has been strong, used assonance, among other varieties of near rhyme, as in the poem called "Exposure":

Our brains ache, in the merciless iced east winds that knive
    us . . .
Wearied we keep awake because the night is silent . . .
Low, drooping flares confuse our memory of the salient . . .
Worried by silence, sentries whisper, curious, nervous,
             But nothing happens.

The word "awake" in the second line is an assonantal rhyme to "brains" in the first line and to "flares" and "salient" in the third; it rhymes fully with "ache" in the first line, which forms assonances with all the other words mentioned. The words "iced, knive, night, silent" in the first two lines are echoed by the further assonance "silence" in the fourth line. There are obviously other echoes here. Thomas deftly employs assonance as a substitute for both internal and end rhyme in his "Poem on his birthday":

             the closer I move
    To death, one man through his sundered hulks,
    The louder the sun blooms
    And the tusked, ramshackling sea exults . . .

There are some full rhymes here: "one" and "sun"; and these are matched with the assonances: "sundered, husks, tusked, exults". There are other assonantal rhymes, notably, "to, move, through, blooms; man, and", as well as the double assonance in "ramshackling". The stressed vowels in the words "louder" and "closer" contribute further to the melody.

Consonance is the pairing of words in which the final consonants of the stressed syllables agree but the vowels differ. This device has also been called CONSONANTAL ASSONANCE, CONSONAN-

TAL RHYME, CONSONANTAL DISSONANCE, DISSONANCE, HALF RHYME, OBLIQUE RHYME, and SUSPENDED RHYME. These terms are the more confusing because some of them are also used for other strategies or for definite kinds of consonance. Thus, half rhyme and more aptly dissonance describe the variation in the vowel sounds in one or more lines, especially when the difference is so slight as to suggest assonance, as in the opening of Hopkins' "The Windhover":

I caught this morning morning's minion, kingdom of daylight's
    dauphin, dapple-dawn-drawn Falcon, in his riding
    Of the rolling level underneath him steady air . . .

Again, suspended rhyme is another term for ANALYZED RHYME, discussed below, and could be used for such delayed dim echoes as are heard in these lines by Edmund Wilson:

Song that pours plaintive or gay from Schubert's blue-coated
    Vienna:
Lindens and lonely men, millers and brooks and May . . .

The same writer employs a *tour de force* that he calls **amphisbaenic** or **backward rhyme**, illustrated in this quatrain:

But tonight I come lone and belated—
Foreseeing in every detail,
And resolved for a day to sidestep
My friends and their guests and their pets.

Disregarding the vowels, José Garcia Villa earlier used this method of rhyming, calling it **reversed consonance**. When the consonance is complete but the vowels do not rhyme, the effect is sometimes called **consonantal dissonance**, sometimes **double consonance**. Examples of this complete consonance are frequent in the work of Hopkins, Dylan Thomas, and Wilfred Owen.

The terminal words in four lines by this last poet will illustrate it:

Pale flakes with fingering stealth come feeling for our faces—
We cringe in holes, back on forgotten dreams, and stare, snow-
    dazed,
Deep into grassier ditches. So we drowse, sun-dozed,
Littered with blossoms trickling where the blackbird fusses.

In some war poems in which he uses consonance Owen follows a higher pitched vowel with a lower pitched one, with grim effectiveness, thus:

> It seemed that out of battle I escaped
> Down some profound dull tunnel, long since scooped
> Through granites which titanic wars had groined.
> Yet also there encumbered sleepers groaned, . . .

John Crowe Ransom uses consonance with particular skill, as in this stanza from his "Judith of Bethulia":

The heathen are all perished. The victory was furnished,
We smote them hiding in our vineyards, barns, annexes,
And now their white bones clutter the holes of foxes,
And the chieftain's head, with grinning sockets, and varnished—
Is it hung on the sky with a hideous epitaphy?
No, the woman keeps the trophy.

Vowel rhyme, in which any vowel is allowed to agree with any other, is rare, though examples can be found, notably in the verse of Emily Dickinson. She compensated for the regularity of her metrics by her unorthodox procedures in the matter of rhyme. These are too various and idiosyncratic to discuss, but one of her quatrains may be cited to illustrate the use of vowel rhyme:

> Nature sometimes rears a sapling,
> Sometimes scalps a tree;
> Her green people recollect it
> When they do not die . . .

An admired artifice in twentieth-century verse is **apocopated rhyme,** so called because the end of one rhyming word is cut off. Long before it was employed by sophisticated poets, it was a feature of balladry, as in these lines:

> Fly around, my pretty little Miss,
> Fly around, I say,
> Fly around, my pretty little Miss,
> You'll drive me almost crazy.

MacLeish uses it to good effect in "Conquistador":

> He with his famous history of New Spain—
> This priest is a learned man: is not ignorant:
> And I am poor: without gold: gainless: . . .

It is apparently impossible to reproduce in English the elaborate arrangement of vowels and consonants demanded by the strict rules of what the Welsh call CYNGHANEDD (pronounced kunhánneth). Nevertheless, in a line from "The Wreck of the *Deutschland*" Hopkins seems to have approximated this scheme: "The down-dugged ground-hugged grey". Not seldom he used the **linked rhyme** found in early Welsh verse. Such rhyme is formed by linking the final syllable in one line with the first sound of the next. Several instances occur in that same poem, as in the following example, the third line running over to the fourth in order to rhyme with the first line:

> She drove in the dark to leeward,
> She struck—not a reef or a rock

But the combs of a smother of sand: night drew her
   Dead to the Kentish Knock . . .

Nothing in English verse quite equals the elaboration of **analyzed rhyme.** True to its name, it must be analyzed to be fully appreciated. Given a quatrain, the vowels of the end-rhymes in the first and third lines are identical, as are those in the second and fourth lines; while the consonants of the end-rhymes in the first and fourth lines are identical, as are those in the second and third lines: This stanza by Auden will illustrate its complexity:

That night when joy began
Our narrowest veins to flush,
We waited for the flash
Of morning's levelled gun.

The rhyming vowels are "beg*a*n : fl*a*sh" and "fl*u*sh : g*u*n". The rhyming consonants are "bega*n* : gu*n*" and "flu*sh* : fla*sh*". Such a *tour de force* is of course unusual. So too is Richard Wilbur's skilful use of alliteration, assonance, consonance, and cross-rhyme in a lyric which opens thus:

These children playing at statues fill
The gardens with their shrillness; in a planned
And planted grove they fling from the swinger's hand
Across the giddy grass and then hold still

In gargoyle attitudes,—as if
All definition were outrageous. Then
They melt in giggles and begin again . . .

In any event, from the earliest rough approximations of rhyme to the most recent sophisticated elaborations of this device, it has been serviceable to good craftsmen. Certainly in the verse of twentieth-century poets no less than in Samuel Daniel's reasoned "Defence of Ryme", published about 1603, it "is demonstratively prooved that Ryme is the fittest harmonie of words that comportes with our Language". Perhaps that is why it is sometimes used as a synonym for verse or poetry.

rhyme royal   See **stanza**, page 169.

rhyme scheme   The pattern of rhymes in a stanza. See **stanza**. See also **rhyme**.

rhythm   As natural as breathing, the pulse of the blood, the ebb and flow of tides, it is immediately experienced and recognized with pleasure, but it eludes definition. Rhythm is perceived in a sequence of events when they recur so regularly that the time intervals they occupy are felt to be either nearly equal to one another or symmetrical. The experience is tinged with emotion and often affords a sense of balance.

Rhythm is so insistent a demand of the organism that the ear finds it, and often elaborates it, in the steady beating of a drum, the ticking of a clock, the chugging of a motor. What is heard as a series of recurring strokes or sensed as a sequence of equal temporal periods satisfies a craving of which the listener may not be aware. Plato said that the life of man in every part has need of it. That necessity governs the motions of a man using an oar, a scythe, a hammer, as those of one wielding a baton. It has given rise to sea chanteys and more primitive work-songs, to lullabies and singing games. If falling into rhythm makes work easier, play jollier, and sleep more seductive, the tendency would seem to have a physiological basis. So it does, as has been borne out by laboratory experiments of some refinement, and duly noted by poets and prosodists.

In speech, be it good prose or verse, rhythm functions overtly and with particular cogency. In verse, each time interval in a sequence is occupied by syllables and pauses, and is usually marked by a beat. O. W. Holmes, a physician as well as a maker of verses, suggested that verse stress is related to pulse beat, and claimed that the rate of a poet's respiration influences the length of his lines, which may account for the difference between the rhythms of Homer and of Herrick. Since the syllables that compose English words vary in pitch as do tones in music, and also in length and accent, these elements affect, to hamper or to help, the rhythm of our verse. Great virtuosos are apt to develop a characteristic one of their own, so that it is natural to speak of a Miltonic or a Yeatsian rhythm. This individual rhythm depends in part on the poet's use of pauses and largely on the nature of his vocabulary: whether like Milton's it abounds in Latinate polysyllables, like that of Frost it sticks close to plain speech, or like Eliot's it moves more freely than either between the pedantic and the popular.

The word "rhythm" is derived from a Greek word meaning "flow", but it is measured flow. RHYME may have the same derivation, or it may be related to an Old Germanic word meaning number or sequence. Whether or not rhyme and rhythm are etymologically kindred, these two elements of verse are intimately linked. When Milton cast rhyme aside as unworthy of his great Argument in *Paradise Lost,* he ignored the fact that this device calls attention to prominent rhythmical periods. Milton contrived to have the pause at the end of a phrase perform a similar service in his blank verse, the phrases being apparently, though not actually, equal in duration. Rhyme, then, emphasizes rhythm but is no more necessary to it than METRE is.

Shelley's "occasional disregard of metre" is noted by a venerable prosodist who hastens to say that he is far from impeaching the poet's rhythm. Metrical verse organizes rhythm in some specific and formal pattern. Such patterns contribute to the grace or dignity of the verse or, in the hands of a W. S. Gilbert or a W. H. Auden, may tickle us. They are not, like rhythm, essential to a poem.

When the metrical scheme is in feet of two syllables the rhythm of the line is **duple**, as in Yeats's line, "Irish / poets, / learn your / trade".

When the metrical scheme requires a three-syllable foot, the rhythm is **triple**, as in Kipling's "For the strength / of the Pack / is the Wolf, / and the strength / of the Wolf / is the Pack."

When the stress falls on the last syllable of a foot, the rhythm is a **rising** one, as in Bridges' "And óff, with a whírr of wíngs", and indeed in most English verse.

When the stress falls on the first syllable of the foot, the rhythm is a **falling** one, as in Brontë's "Héavy and dárk the níght is clósing".

When the stress falls between two unstressed syllables, as in this line of Swinburne's: "Far óut to the shállows and stráits of the fúture, by róugh ways or pléasant", the rhythm is a **rocking** one.

Metres in which stressed and unstressed syllables alternate, duple rhythm rising or falling, exhibit **running** or **common rhythm**. This is not to be confused with COMMON MEASURE. The types of rhythm are few as compared to the wide variety of metrical schemes. No one would question the energetic rhythm of the following passages, though no two of them could be scanned alike.

> Warriors and Chiefs! should the shaft or the sword
> Pierce me in leading the host of the Lord,
> Heed not the corse, though a King's in your path:
> Bury your steel in the bosoms of Gath!
>
> BYRON

> We trenched, we trumpeted and drummed,
> And from our mortars tons of iron hummed

Ath'art the ditch, the month we bombed
The town o' Valencieën.

HARDY

I lo'e the stishie
O' Earth in space
Breengin' by
At a haliket pace.

A wecht o' hills
Gangs wallopin' owre.
Syne a whummlin' sea
Wi' a gallus glower . . .

MACDIARMID

Concern for rhythmical liberties has resulted in the development of SPRUNG RHYTHM and FREE VERSE, each of which is discussed in its appropriate place. Both, rejecting an abstract metrical scheme, to which the speech rhythm is subordinate, seek to reconcile the natural speech stresses with the fluent character of a phrase in music. Rhythmical prose, when it is not disagreeably close to metrical verse and when the language is fit, approaches poetry. Rhythm does not suffice to turn a literary work into a poem, but it is very nearly as essential to poetry as breathing is to life. The tempo of the lines may be fast or slow, they may be rich or poor in imagery, they may observe strictly the rules of metrics or follow relatively loose cadences, but, except where the poem is concrete, and not seldom then as well, they must be rhythmical: they must give the listener a sense that syllables and pauses fill equal or symmetrical temporal periods, which recur with pleasing regularity. This is one of the ways in which the poem, which may

Be of a man skating, a woman dancing, a woman
Combing . . .

provides, in Wallace Stevens' words,

. . . the finding of a satisfaction.

rhythmical pause One that separates phrases when the speaker draws breath. Not counted as part of the metrical pattern, in the reading of verse with a strongly marked rhythm it tends to create a singsong effect.

rich rhyme See **rhyme**, page 131.

rime See **rhyme**.

rime couée See **stanza**, page 169.

rime riche See **rhyme**, page 131.

rising rhythm See **rhythm**, page 144.

rocking rhythm See **rhythm**, page 144.

romance Although the word now applies also to prose, it signifies particularly a chivalric tale in verse, such as, or similar to, the cycle of Arthurian legends.

> While Romance could charm,
> The world gave ground before her bright array;

wrote Byron, declaring, however, that "Cervantes smiled Spain's chivalry away" and presumably not Spain's only. Yet at the same time Keats was beholding

> upon the night's starred face,
> Huge cloudy symbols of a high romance . . .

romantic A term used of poetry that is centered upon the inner rather than upon the outer world, that tries to convey the poet's feelings in a manner uniquely expressive of his experience and his personality, and that is not bound by traditional patterns. These features distinguish it from classical poetry. The romantic movement that started at the close of the eighteenth

century was a reaction against the formalism of a period domi-
nated by a mechanistic view of life. **Romanticism,** another
name for this reaction, applies also to any trend exalting nature
above artifice, sensibility above intellect, the foreign above the
familiar, energy above restraint, the search for an Absolute above
concern with the here and now. Looking before or after, the
romantic pines for what is not. Francis Scarfe, a poet involved
with a recent romantic movement, said truly that "it is impossible to talk about Romanticism and Classicism long without
talking nonsense." Yet no one would mistake Landor for anything but a classical poet or Tom Moore for anything but a romantic one, as in our own time was Dylan Thomas, for whom
song was "a burning and crested act . . .". See also **romantic
irony,** page 72.

romantic irony   See **irony.**

romanticism   See **romantic.**

rondeau   This has come to be the usual term for one of the
French forms similar to the RONDEL, with which it was at one
time synonymous. The rondeau is more frequently used. It
consists of thirteen lines divided into three stanzas, all on two
rhymes, and an unrhymed refrain to the second and third stanzas
formed from the opening words of the first line. The refrain is
in effect a tail and is often a pun. The first and last stanzas are
of five lines; the second stanza of three, and the metre is normally
tetrameter. With R signifying the refrain, the scheme is *a a b b a,
a a b R, a a b b a R,* as in this rondeau by Henley:

> Let us be drunk, and for a while forget,
> Forget, and, ceasing even from regret,
> Live without reason and despite of rhyme,
> As in a dream preposterous and sublime,
> Where place and hour and means for once are met.

Where is the use of effort? Love and debt
And disappointment have us in a net.
Let us break out, and taste the morning prime . . .
        Let us be drunk.

In vain our little hour we strut and fret,
And mouth our wretched parts as for a bet:
We cannot please the tragicaster Time.
To gain the crystal sphere, the silver clime,
Where Sympathy sits dimpling on us yet,
        Let us be drunk!

The rondeau may also consist of ten lines, of which the scheme
is *a b b a a b R, a b b a R*, as in this example from Villon translated by John Payne:

Death, of thy rigour I complain,
    That hast my lady torn from me,
    And yet wilt not contented be,
Till from me too all strength be ta'en
For languishment of heart and brain.
    What harm did she in life to thee,
        Death?

One heart we had betwixt us twain;
    Which being dead, I too must dree
Death, or like carven saints we see
In choir, sans life to live be fain,
        Death!

The **rondeau redoublé**, distantly related to the rondeau proper,
is a more elaborate form, consisting of six quatrains on two alternating rhymes, with a strict pattern of recurrent lines throughout, the first half of the initial line being repeated as an unrhymed tail to the last stanza. Each line of the first quatrain

serves, in order; as the last line of the four succeeding quatrains, the rhyme scheme and the tail linking the final stanza with the first. The pattern is A B A' B' , b a b A , a b a B , b a b A' , a b a B' , b a b a R . Dorothy Parker wrote a rondeau redoublé with the sub-title "And Scarcely Worth the Trouble", of which the first, second, and final stanzas follow:

> The same to me are sombre days and gay.
>> Though joyous dawns the rosy morn, and bright,
> Because my dearest love is gone away
>> Within my heart is melancholy night.
>
> My heart beats low in loneliness, despite
>> That riotous Summer holds the earth in sway.
> In cerements my spirit is bedight;
>> The same to me are sombre days and gay.
>
> And this, O love, my pitiable plight
>> Whenever from my circling arms you stray;
> This little world of mine has lost its light . . .
>> I hope to God, my dear, that you can say
>>> The same to me.

The **rondel** is a poem of fourteen lines on two rhymes with a re-frain, the first two lines of the opening quatrain recurring at the close of the second quatrain and that of the concluding sestet. The metre varies, as does the rhyme scheme, a frequent arrange-ment being A B b a , a b A B , a b b a A B . Occasionally the rondel is shortened to thirteen lines, one line of the refrain being omitted from the last stanza. **Roundel,** although the Chaucerian spelling of rondel, for which he used a refrain of three lines, is the name now commonly reserved for the variant invented by Swinburne. Its structure is three tercets on two rhymes and a refrain taken from the opening of the first line and rhyming with the second line. With R signifying this rhymed refrain, the scheme is *a b a R , b a b , a b a R* . The metre varies from one roundel to another. Swinburne at once describes and illustrates the form:

A Roundel is wrought as a ring or a starbright sphere,
With craft of delight and with cunning of sound unsought,
That the heart of the hearer may smile if to pleasure his ear
      A roundel is wrought.

Its jewel of music is carven of all or of aught—
Love, laughter, or mourning—remembrance or rapture or fear—
That fancy may fashion to hang in the ear of thought.

As a bird's quick song runs round, and the hearts in us hear—
Pause answers to pause, and again the same strain caught,
So moves the device whence, round as a pearl or tear,
      A roundel is wrought.

The **triolet** is in the nature of a little rondel, consisting of two quatrains on two rhymes, the first line being repeated as the fourth and seventh, and the second line repeated as the last. The scheme is *A B a A a b A B* . This example is by Hardy:

    How great my grief, my joys how few,
    Since first it was my fate to know thee!
    —Have the slow years not brought to view
    How great my grief, my joys how few,
    Nor memory shaped old times anew,
      Nor loving-kindness helped to show thee
    How great my grief, my joys how few,
      Since first it was my fate to know thee?

rondeau redoublé   See **rondeau**, page 149.

rondel   See **rondeau**, page 149.

roundel   See **rondeau,** page 149.

rubaiyat   This is the Persian word for quatrains (ruba'ai is the singular form), the equal lines consisting of three or four feet, rhyming *a a b a* . Because of the fame of Fitzgerald's version of the rubaiyat of Omar Khayyám, the structure has come to be called the Omar stanza. The ruba'ai is an independent lyric, not a member of a sequence forming a long poem; the continuity of the *Rubaiyat* that we know was bestowed upon the verses by the translator. A recent example of the form occurs in Pound's *Pisan Cantos,* where it is used at the close of Canto LXXX in a poem of three stanzas, this being the second:

> Nor seeks the carmine petal to infer;
> Nor is the white bud Time's inquisitor
> Probing to know if its new-gnarled root
> Twists from York's head or belly of Lancaster.

runes   The letters of the earliest Teutonic alphabet; since these were largely used for incantations, a rune has come to mean a magical formula or poem. Poe heard the bells

> Keeping time, time, time,
> In a sort of Runic rhyme . . .

Kipling composed a set of verses called "The Runes on Weland's Sword" which begins:

> A Smith makes me
> To betray my Man
> In my first fight.

More recently W. S. Merwin wrote a set of "Runes for a Round Table", each of which bore the title of one of the signs of the zodiac. This is the rune for *Sagittarius*:

All quarry flees. The arrow
Drawn always to my ear I still
Have not let fly, and yet they fall.

running rhythm   See **rhythm**, page 144.

run-on line   See **couplet**.

[S]

sapphics   The four-line stanza in the metre associated with the name of the Greek poet Sappho. The term also applies to the metre of the first three lines of the stanza. It was used by the Romans and has been imitated by poets writing in English. This stanza from Swinburne's "Sapphics" exemplifies it well:

> Āll thĕ nīght slēep cāme / nŏt ŭpōn mў̄ eȳelĭds,
> Shēd nŏt dēw, nŏr shōok / nŏr ŭnclōsed ā̆ fēathĕr,
> Yēt wĭth līps shūt clōse / ănd wĭth eȳes ŏf īrŏn
>   Stŏod ănd bĕ / hēld mĕ.

satire   Verse that ridicules a prevailing vice or folly, a person or an institution that the author holds in contempt. The following lines are from Dryden's version of Juvenal's "Satire Against Women":

> A Sober man like thee to change his life!
> What fury would possess thee with a wife?
> Art thou of every other death bereft,
> No knife, no ratbane, no kind halter left?
> (For every noose compar'd to hers is cheap)
> Is there no city bridge from whence to leap?

A satire by John Oldham thus advises the maker of verse:

In fine, turn pettifogger, canonist,
Civilian, pedant, mountebank or priest,
Soldier or merchant, fiddler, painter, fencer,
Jack-pudding, juggler, player or rope-dancer;
Preach, plead, cure, fight, game, pimp, beg, cheat or thieve;
Be all but poet, and there's way to live.

Satire can include such resonant lines as Byron's "Brave men were living before Agamemnon." Nor need it be as forthright as the verses quoted above. Hardy's "Satires of Circumstance" are poems presenting incidents that abruptly reveal the weakness, stupidity, or cruelty of the speaker or the person spoken of. See also **Hudibrastic verse.**

scald   A Scandinavian bard in ancient times. Longfellow introduces "The Saga of King Olaf" with reference to

> Legends in the old Norse tongue,
> Of the dead kings of Norroway,—
> Legends that once were told or sung
> In many a smoky fireside nook
> Of Iceland, in the ancient day,
> By wandering Saga-man or Scald . . .

scansion   The detailed analysis of the metrical pattern of lines and stanzas. The terms employed are those of classical prosody. Some of them, notably those connected with the practice of beating time, are useful in discussing English metrical verse. Other terms are awkward and a few are confusing, the more so because Greek and Latin usage sometimes differed. That the rules of quantitative verse are inapplicable to our own is acknowledged; the technical jargon persists. Custom has forced its acceptance upon those who kick against its inadequacy. The difference between the CLASSICAL HEXAMETER, which is in duple time, and the ENGLISH HEXAMETER, which is in triple

time, is one instance; the confusion over ARSIS and THESIS furnishes another. When a line of verse fits a certain metre awk-
wardly, it is said that the line does not scan. The same line
may conform to another metrical scheme, and read in accordance with it the line will scan. Further, unless or until the
metre is established, the reader may be mistaken as to the
proper scansion of a line. This line of Scott's read out of context would be scanned as trochaic tetrameter: "Cālm ănd /
sĭlĕnt, / dārk ănd / deēp". Patmore showed that the dactylic
metre of the preceding lines set the norm for this one, and
so it must be scanned the same way. Rests compensate for the
omitted syllables.

Mērrĭlў / swĭm wĕ; thĕ / moōn ˄ shĭnes / brĭght:˄ ˄
Dŏwnwărd wĕ / drĭft thrŏugh thĕ / shădŏw ănd / lĭght:˄ ˄
Ūndĕr yŏur / rōck ˄ thĕ / eēdĭes ˄ / sleēp˄ ˄
Cālm ˄ ănd / sĭlĕnt, ˄ / dārk ˄ănd / deēp.˄ ˄

Even where there is no doubt as to the metre of a line there
may be diverse opinions as to the correct scansion. Laboratory
studies in the reading of verse show that prosodists of the old
school tended to ignore certain physical and psychological
factors that affect timing. Conventional scansion does not give
a true account of the facts. As Thomas Parkinson has well said,
Yeats "knew nothing about scansion, but everything about
versification." See also **compensation; metre; prosodic symbols;
substitution.**

secondary accent   See **accent.**

sense stress   See **metre,** page 88.

sensibility   The receptive, responsive awareness that characterizes a poet and helps the reader to an understanding of a

poem. When Coleridge opined that "deep thinking is attainable only by a man of deep feeling" and that "the souls of five hundred Sir Isaac Newtons would go to the making up of a Shakspere . . .", he was contrasting the quality of their respective sensibilities. DISSOCIATION OF SENSIBILITY is a term coined by Eliot for the character of poetry influenced by the eighteenth-century view that thought and feeling are not intimately related.

septenary   A seven-foot line. See also **metre**, page 87.

sestet   A poem or stanza of six lines, the term most frequently referring to the second part of a sonnet.

sestina   An elaborate form, originating in Provence and imported into English verse from Italy, it consists of six stanzas, of six lines each, with a concluding tercet. It is usually unrhymed but the end words of the first stanza impose a pattern analogous to a rhyme scheme, since they are all repeated in the succeeding stanzas in a strict order that varies with each stanza and they recur in the tercet. With the numbers 1, 2, 3, 4, 5, 6 representing the end words of the initial stanza, and each line representing a stanza, the scheme may be set down thus:

$$1, 2, 3, 4, 5, 6$$
$$6, 1, 5, 2, 4, 3$$
$$3, 6, 4, 1, 2, 5$$
$$5, 3, 2, 6, 1, 4$$
$$4, 5, 1, 3, 6, 2$$
$$2, 4, 6, 5, 3, 1$$
$$5, 3, 1$$

In order to include in the tercet the end words 2, 4, 6, these are used either at the start or in the middle of the lines. This difficult form has been used by Swinburne and Kipling, and with symbolic significance by Auden in a poem of which the first stanza follows:

"We have brought you," they said, "a map of the country;
Here is the line that runs to the vats,
This patch of green on the left is the wood,
We've pencilled an arrow to point out the bay,
No thank you, no tea; why look at the clock.
Keep it? Of course. It goes with our love."

The tercet is unconventional as befits a poem that has been
called "an attack on habit and docility", the end words being
4, 2, 6, preceded by 3, 5, 1:

> Sees water in the wood and trees by the bay,
> Hears a clock striking near the vats;
> "This is your country and the home of love."

Shakespearean sonnet   See **sonnet,** page 161.

short couplet   See **couplet,** page 38.

short measure   See **common measure.**

simile   See **metaphor,** page 82.

sirvente   See **troubadour,** page 183.

Skeltonic verse   The stressed verse used so effectively by
John Skelton, the tutor of the prince who became Henry VIII.
Skelton paid no heed to the number of syllables in his lines,
which were often short ones of two stresses or three, and he
added emphasis by both alliteration and rhyme. In "Colin
Clout" he wrote justly of his own verse:

> And if ye stand in doubt
> Who brought this about,
> My name is Colin Clout.
> I purpose to shake out
> All my conning bag.
> Like a clerkly hag,

> For though my rhyme be ragged,
> Tatteréd and jaggéd,
> Rudely rain-beaten,
> Rusty and moth-eaten,
> If ye take well therewith,
> It hath in it some pith.

This ragged rhyme is also called **tumbling verse.** The Scotch poet-king, James VI, declared it fit only for satirical poems. Lines so written, he observed, "be out of ordour, and keipis na kynde nor reule of Flowing and for that cause are callit Tumbling verse . . .". Spenser used it in his "Shepheardes Calender" to create an atmosphere of rude rusticity, as in these lines, each having four stresses but varying from one another in the number of their syllables:

> O thou greate shepheard, Lobbin, how great is thy griefe!
> The colourd chaplets, wrought with a chiefe,
> The knotted rushringes, and gilte rosemaree?
> For shee deemed nothing too deere for thee.

The lines that follow, excerpts from "Homage to John Skelton", contradict James VI's condemnation.

> Your name is Parrot: "a bird of Paradise"?
> In Heaven, they say, Hebrew is the Word,
> While you use every language, naughty or nice,
> Greek, Latin, Welsh as you were Dylan's bird,
> Italian, Castilian—good Skelton you've skirred
> Hither thither hardily, but, spoken or sung,
> Harsh or silk-soft, yours is the English tongue.

> *　　*　　*　　*

> You had only to call,
> The words came, one and all,

The tiny words, the tall,
The fragrant, the fresh
As a fine peach's flesh
Or silken purse's mesh.
Nor you did not disdain
The shaggy words, the plain
And nasty, as though they'd lain
Nightlong out in the rain . . .

You made poems with words
Like all sagacious birds.
And if your rhythms go tumbling,
Bumbling and rumbling,
So that some grumble,
Declaring you fumble,
Then their wits are numb
As a frostbitten thumb
That can pick up no crumb.

slant rhyme   See **rhyme**, page 131.

S.M.   An abbreviation for short measure.

sonnet   Normally a poem of fourteen iambic pentameter lines, divided into an octave and a sestet, with a prescribed rhyme scheme, and concerned with a single thought or sentiment. Originating in Provence, the particular form called the Italian sonnet was perfected by Petrarch and therefore is also known as Petrarchan. Its OCTAVE is rhymed *a b b a a b b a*, the SESTET is on two or three rhymes, distinct from those in the octave, and while various arrangements are accepted, those commonly used are *c d c d c d , c d e c d e , c d e d c e* . The octave presents the theme in the first quatrain and develops it in the second; the sestet exemplifies or reflects upon it in the first TERCET and brings it to a logical emphatic close in the second.

The Italian form has been used by poets writing in English, but rarely with the complete fidelity of the following example by Dante Gabriel Rossetti:

The gloom that breathes upon me with these airs
    Is like the drops which strike the traveller's brow
    Who knows not, darkling, if they bring him now
Fresh storm, or be old rain the covert bears.
Ah! bodes this hour some harvest of new tares,
    Or hath but memory of the day whose plough
    Sowed hunger once,—the night at length when thou,
O prayer found vain, didst fall from out my prayers?

How prickly were the growths which yet how smooth,
    Along the hedgerows of this journey shed,
    Lie by Time's grace till night and sleep may soothe!
    Even as the thistledown from pathsides dead
Gleaned by a girl in autumns of her youth,
    Which one new year makes soft her marriage-bed.

This is part of a group of sonnets called *The House of Life*. The earliest of such SONNET SEQUENCES in English is Sidney's *Astrophel and Stella*. A contemporary example may be found in Auden's *The Quest*.

The **English** or **Shakespearean sonnet** allows for a break between octave and sestet but is composed of three quatrains, each with different pairs of rhymes, and a final couplet, independently rhymed, which makes an effective climax: *a b a b, c d c d, e f e f, g g*, as in Shakespeare's seventy-third sonnet:

That time of yeare thou maist in me behold,
When yellow leaves, or none, or few doe hange
Upon those boughes which shake against the could,
Bare ruin'd quiers, where late the sweet birds sang.
In me thou seest the twi-light of such day,

As after Sun-set fadeth in the West,
Which by and by blacke night doth take away,
Deaths second selfe that seals up all in rest.
In me thou seest the glowing of such fire,
That on the ashes of his youth doth lye,
As the death bed, where on it must expire,
Consum'd with that which it was nurrisht by.
This thou percev'st, which makes thy love more strong,
To love that well, which thou must leave ere long.

Spenser employed a rhyme scheme which links octave and sestet and concludes with an independently rhymed couplet: *a b a b-b c b c c d c d , e e* , a form know as the **Spenserian sonnet:**

Lacking my love, I go from place to place,
Like a young fawn that late hath lost the hind,
And seek each where, where last I saw her face,
Whose image yet I carry fresh in mind.
I seek the fields with her late footing signed;
I seek her bower with her late presence decked;
Yet nor in field nor bower I her can find;
Yet field and bower are full of her aspèct:
But when mine eyes I thereunto direct,
They idly back return to me again:
And when I hope to see their true objèct,
I find myself but fed with fancies vain.
    Cease then, mine eyes, to seek her self to see;
    And let my thoughts behold her self in me.

Milton contrived a form that keeps the rhyme scheme of the Petrarchan octave but does not admit the customary break in the sense at the start of the sestet, so that the structure is a more unified whole, as this **Miltonic sonnet** shows:

When I consider how my light is spent,
E're half my days, in this dark world and wide,
And that one Talent which is death to hide,
Lodg'd with me useless, though my Soul more bent
To serve therewith my Maker, and present
My true account, least he returning chide,
Doth God exact day-labour, light deny'd,
I fondly ask; But patience to prevent
That murmur, soon replies, God doth not need
Either man's work or his own gifts, who best
Bear his mild yoak, they serve him best, his State
Is Kingly. Thousands at his bidding speed
And post o're Land and Ocean without rest:
They also serve who only stand and waite.

He also composed a so-called **tailed sonnet**, "On the new Forcers
of Conscience", running to twenty lines, of which the additional
ones have been called the tail, although, properly speaking, only
the shorter are tails. The rhyme scheme of the sestet is $c\,d\,e\,$-
$d\,e\,c$; that of the six added lines will be seen to be $c\,f\,f\,f\,g\,g$:

But we do hope to find out all your tricks,
Your plots and packing wors then those of *Trent*,
That so the Parliament
May with their wholsom and preventive Shears
Clip your Phylacteries, though bauk your Ears,
And succour our just Fears
When they shall read this clearly in your charge
New Presbyter is but *Old Priest* writ Large.

Wordsworth, a great sonneteer, took further liberties with the
Italian form, including the occasional use of $a\,c\,c\,a$ in the second
quatrain. The variations on the sonnet are too many to illustrate
or even to discuss. The experiments of Hopkins include several

in sprung rhythm, one of which, "the longest sonnet ever made",
has eight stresses to a line. It begins:

Earnest, earthless, equal, atuneable, / vaulty, voluminous . . .
         stupendous
Evening strains to be time's vast, / womb-of-all, home-of-all,
       hearse-of-all night.

He also designed what he called a "CURTAL SONNET", which
opens with a sestet, rhyming *a b c a b c*, and concludes with a
quatrain and tail, rhyming *d b c d c* or *d c b d c*. The form is
exemplified in "Pied Beauty":

Glory be to God for dappled things—
    For skies of couple-colour as a brinded cow;
        For rose-moles all in stipple upon trout that swim;
Fresh-firecoal chestnut-falls, finches' wings;
    Landscape plotted and pieced—fold, fallow, and plough;
        And all trades, their gear and tackle and trim.

All things counter, original, spare, strange;
    Whatever is fickle, freckled (who knows how?)
        With swift, slow; sweet, sour; adazzle, dim;
He Fathers-forth whose beauty is past change:
           Praise him.

Elinor Wylie wrote what she called a "Little Sonnet" presumably because, although octave and sestet are complete, the
lines are tetrameters. In "The Silken Tent" Frost composed a
sonnet which is a single sentence. The tireless contemporary
sonneteer, Merrill Moore, handled the form with freedom in
both his rhyme schemes and his metres, as illustrated here:

    There was a moon, a young one in the sky
    And a cold breeze blowing from the upper air

And a rapid creek flowing not far from where
The salt lick was, where all the sheep were bedded
In the white moonlight I could see to read by
Were I a literary shepherd wedded
To printed pastorals instead of the natural ones
Ruled over by sun and moon and stars and seasons.

Shepherds that really cared about their sheep
Would never have left them out of doors to sleep
On such a night as this; they might be bewitched
And grow with spotted hides and poor-grade wool,

Valuable sheep always should be watched
And allowed to breed only when the moon is full.

sonnet sequence   See **sonnet,** page 161.

Spenserian sonnet   See **sonnet,** page 161.

Spenserian stanza   See **stanza,** page 169.

spondaic   See **metre,** page 88. See also **free verse,** page 56.

spondee   A foot of two syllables, both long or stressed. See **metre,** page 88.

sprung rhythm   Used of verse in which the line is measured by the number of stresses, each coinciding with the natural speech stress, which is given particular emphasis. The name was coined by Gerard Manley Hopkins, its most famous practitioner, because the effect of the rhythm seems abrupt in contrast to the smooth flow of the running rhythm common to English verse in his time. This abruptness is marked when stresses crowd upon one another, as a line by Hopkins illustrates: "The héart rears wíngs bóld and bólder". Running rhythm forbids such juxtaposition of stresses. Another difference is that running rhythm affords the possibility of making the speech stresses run

counter to those of the strict metrical scheme. The effect is
clear in this line of a poem composed in iambic pentameter:
"The gaiety of language is our seigneur". The abstract metrical
pattern, which here serves as a foil for the speech cadence, is
absent from a poem in sprung rhythm. Hopkins was concerned with giving an account in conventional terms of his
departures from orthodox prosody and he also invented a terminology and used his own symbols for some of the liberties that
he took. Thus to slack or unstressed syllables not counted in a
foot he gave the name "hanger" or "outride". The mark for
this occurs in the opening line of his "Hurrahing in Harvest":

Summer énds now; nów bárbarous in beáuty, the stóoks arise
Around . . .

Making his plea for a rhythm neglected or maligned since Spenser's time, Hopkins declared it to be "the rhythm of common
speech and of written prose, when rhythm is perceived in them"
and "of all but the most monotonously regular music". He found
it also in nursery rhymes and in such Middle English verse as
Piers Plowman. Indeed, the devices of Old and Middle English
verse, such as alliteration, assonance, consonantal emphasis,
which help to mark sense-stress, are natural to poems written
according to this principle. Free verse excepted, sprung rhythm
is closer to music than is any other form of verse. In the hands
of so conscientious a craftsman as Hopkins, it is more scrupu-
lously timed than free verse. It often exhibits some of the characteristics of metrical verse, such as the predominance in a poem
of some specific foot, and the use of an elaborate stanzaic form
with a pattern of resonant rhymes. Unlike Whitman, whom the
vers librists claimed as an "Ancestor" and whose free cadences
Hopkins declared closely akin to his own, he worked consciously
with or against the rules of conventional metrics. That the ma-

jority of his poems are sonnets, albeit often unorthodox ones, is final evidence of the discipline that he accepted along with the freedom that sprung rhythm has to offer. A stanza from his lyric on "Inversnaid" exemplifies it:

> This darksome burn, horseback brown,
> His rollrock highroad roaring down,
> In coop and in comb the fleece of his foam
> Flutes and low to the lake falls home.

The lines may be contrasted with Wordsworth's reference to the same spot in his address "To a Highland Girl, at Inversneyde, upon Loch Lomond":

> This fall of water that doth make
> A murmur near the silent lake . . .

Blake's "To the Evening Star" has more than once been cited as approximating sprung rhythm:

> Thou fair-hair'd angel of the evening,
> Now, whilst the sun rests on the mountains, light
> Thy bright torch of love; thy radiant crown
> Put on, and smile upon our evening bed!
> Smile on our loves, and, while thou drawest the
> Blue curtains of the sky, scatter thy silver dew
> On every flower that shuts its sweet eyes
> In timely sleep. Let thy west wind sleep on
> The lake; speak silence with thy glimmering eyes,
> And wash the dusk with silver. Soon, full soon,
> Dost thou withdraw; then the wolf rages wide,
> And the lion glares thro' the dun forest;
> The fleece of our flocks are cover'd with
> Thy sacred dew; protect them with thine influence.

Hopkins said that Blake was one of those who "took up Sprung Rhythm and mislaid it again".

stand   See **ode**, page 107.

stanza   Lines of verse grouped so as to compose a pattern that is usually repeated in the poem. Its distinguishing features are the number of lines, the number of feet or stresses in each line, and the rhyme scheme. As a rhetorical unit the stanza when short has been compared to a sentence and when long to a paragraph. It is also a melodic unit. On the well-supported theory that our vowels correspond to the steps of the chromatic scale, Henry Lanz defines the stanza as "a specific system of melodic tensions and relaxations caused by some specific arrangement of the vowel-keys". **Stave** is another name for stanza, suggestive of its association with song. STROPHE, also synonymous with stanza, usually is reserved for part of an ode, which may be irregular in form, or to a division of a poem in free verse.

The usual way to indicate the structure of a stanza is to use the same small letter of the alphabet for all lines rhyming with each other, placing above each letter an arabic numeral like an exponent to represent the number of feet or stresses in the line. When successive lines of a stanza are of the same length, the numeral is placed above the last letter in the series. Lines repeated in their entirety are represented by capital letters. The structure of all but three stanzas of Lewis Carroll's "Jabberwocky" would be represented as this one is:

> "Beware the Jabberwock, my son! a^4
> The jaws that bite, the claws that catch! b^4
> Beware the Jubjub bird, and shun a^4
> The frumious Bandersnatch!" b^3

In the first and third lines of the three other stanzas the end rhyme is lacking, so that those stanzas would be represented thus: $a\ b\ c^4\ b^3$

Certain stanza forms are named for the poets who invented them or with whose work they are closely associated. Thus Spenser's elaboration of an iambic pentameter group by adding the majesty of an alexandrine is called the **Spenserian stanza:** $a\ b\ a\ b\ b\ c\ b\ c^5\ c^6$. It has been used effectively by later crafts-men, as here by Byron:

> It is the hush of night, and all between
> Thy margin and the mountains, dusk, yet clear,
> Mellowed and mingling, yet distinctly seen,
> Save darkened Jura, whose capt heights appear
> Precipitously steep; and drawing near,
> There breathes a living fragrance from the shore,
> Of flowers yet fresh with childhood; on the ear
> Drops the light drip of the suspended oar,
> Or chirps the grasshopper one good-night carol more.

Shelley adopted it for "The Revolt of Islam", not because he considered it "a finer model of poetical harmony than the blank verse of Shakespeare or Milton, but because in the latter there is no shelter for mediocrity: you must either succeed or fail".

The Spenserian stanza is one line longer than the **Monk's Tale stanza,** $a\ b\ a\ b\ b\ c\ b\ c^5$, so called because it was used by Chaucer in that verse narrative. The **In Memoriam stanza,** an iambic quatrain, $a\ b\ b\ a^4$, was not invented by Tennyson but he made it famous in the poem for which it is named and from which the lines below are quoted. Because it has enclosing rhymes this is an **envelope stanza.**

> A man upon a stall may find,
>   And, passing, turn the page that tells

> A grief, then changed to something else
> Sung by a long-forgotten mind.

Stanzas are occasionally named for the number of their lines, as the COUPLET which has two, the TERCET and TERZA RIMA which have three, the QUATRAIN which has four, and OTTAVA RIMA which has eight lines. Some of these structures have specific rhyme schemes and metres. An instance is **ottava rima**, as its name indicates an Italian form, consisting of eight iambic pentameter lines, rhyming $a\ b\ a\ b\ a\ b\ c\ c^5$. Auden notes that the rhymes divide it into a group of six lines followed by a couplet and that the poet can either "use this as an epigrammatic comment" on the preceding lines or "take seven lines for his theme and use the final one as a punch line". Byron used the former strategy in *Don Juan*:

> A tigress robb'd of young, a lioness,
> > Or any interesting beast of prey
> Are similes at hand for the distress
> > Of ladies who cannot have their own way;
> But though my turn will not be served with less,
> > These don't express one half what I should say
> For what is stealing young ones, few or many,
> To cutting short their hopes of having any?

Yeats lent the form new dignity in "Sailing to Byzantium" and "Among School Children".

The uses of the quatrain naturally vary with the metre and rhyme scheme employed. It is commonly used in the BALLAD and in the HYMNAL STANZA. **Rhyme royal**, $a\ b\ a\ b\ b\ c\ c^5$, was imported into English verse by Chaucer. Because he used it often and well, notably in his *Troilus and Criseyde*, it is also called the **Chaucer** and the **Troilus stanza**.

> Ye knowe eek, that in forme of speche is chaunge

> With-inne a thousand yeer, and wordes tho
> That hadden prys, now wonder nyce and straunge
> Us thinketh hem; and yet they spake hem so,
> And spedde as wel in love as men now do;
> Eek for to winne love in sondry ages,
> In sondry londes, sondry been usages.

Gascoigne declared it to be surely "a royall kind of verse, serving best for grave discourses". Auden notes that from Chaucer to Sackville it was "the staple vehicle for a long poem", since it calls for only one triple rhyme, while ottava rima calls for two. He apologizes for not having used the latter, which would, he knows, be "The proper instrument on which to pay" his compliments, in his *Letter to Lord Byron*, but affirms that "Rhyme royal's difficult enough to play." Other importations used in more elaborate structures are noted under FRENCH FORMS.

The usual structure of the **tail-rhyme stanza**, often given its French name of **rime couée**, is $a\ a^4\ b^3\ c\ c^4\ b^3$. As the name implies, its chief feature is that a group of lines be followed by a shorter line, like a TAIL to the others, rhyming with another equally short line. The tails are sometimes printed so as to emphasize their brevity. There are a number of variants on this stanza, including some in which, as it were, the tail wags the dog, the isolated rhyming lines being longer than the lines grouped above them. A familiar variant is the **Burns stanza**, $a\ a\ a^4\ b^2\ a^4\ b^2$, exemplified herewith:

> Gie me ae spark o' Nature's fire,
> That's a' the learning I desire;
> Then tho' I drudge thro' dub an' mire
> At pleugh or cart,
> My Muse, though hamely in attire,
> May touch the heart.

Tails or codas to a stanza do not necessarily rhyme with any other line. One or more phrases or lines repeated at the close of every stanza are the **burden** or **refrain**. Such is the last line in this stanza by Thomas Nashe:

> Beauty is but a flowre,
> Which wrinkles will devoure,
> Brightness falls from the ayre,
> Queenes have died yong and faire,
> Dust hath closde *Helens* eye.
> I am sick, I must dye:
> > Lord have mercy on us.

Not part of the litany, but what he properly calls "a Provençal burden", recurs at the close of each stanza of Swinburne's "In the Orchard", which opens thus:

> Leave go my hands, let me catch breath and see;
> Let the dewfall drench either side of me;
> > Clear apple-leaves are soft upon the moon
> Seen sidelong like a blossom on the tree;
> > Ah God, ah God, that day should be so soon.

See also **ballad; common measure; couplet; French forms; ode; rubaiyat; sestina; sonnet; terza rima; Welsh forms.**

stave   See **stanza.**

stichomythia   Dialogue, in alternating lines, marked by antithesis and rhetorical repetition; it is used, as in classical Greek drama, in sharp altercation. This example is from *Hamlet*:

Queen: Hamlet, thou has thy father much offended.
Hamlet: Mother, you have my father much offended.
Queen: Come, come, you answer with an idle tongue.
Hamlet: Go, go, you question with a wicked tongue.

stock response   The habitual response that the uncritical reader makes to the elements of a poem and that to which the conventional versifier appeals.

strategy   The way in which the poet manipulates rhythm, metaphor, stanzaic pattern, together with other technical means, to make his poem the utterance that is required. Ransom defines it as "the structure-texture procedure of poets".

stress   See **metre**, page 88. See also **ictus; thesis**.

stress prosody   See **metre**, page 88.

strophe   See **ode**. See also **stanza**.

structural metaphor   See **metaphor**, page 82.

structure   See **form**. See also **texture**.

subdued metaphor   See **metaphor**, page 82.

substitution   The use of a foot other than that normally required by the metre. The classical rule of **equivalence** makes two short syllables equal to one long. In quantitative verse, therefore, dactyls, anapests, spondees, amphibrachs, and cretics may be substituted for one another. By the same rule, an iamb may be substituted for a trochee and vice versa. This form of substitution, like that of dactyl for an anapest, results in a **reversed** or **inverted foot**. In accentual-syllabic verse the term for such reversal may be **inverted stress** or **accent**. It is illustrated in the first foot of the line by Pope quoted below. The substitution of a trisyllabic foot for the normal one in dissyllabic verse was admitted, however rarely, even by that strict metrist, as the same line shows:

Thrō' thĕ / fāir scēne / rōll slōw / thĕ līng / ĕrĭng strēams . . .

This is obviously not a form of equivalence. See also **compensation; metre**.

suspended rhyme   See **rhyme**, page 131.

syllabic verse   See **metre**, page 88.

symbol   A word or an image that signifies something other than what it represents and that even when denoting a physical, limited thing carries enlarging connotations, so that it has the reality, vivid yet ambiguous, the emotional power, and the suggestiveness of a compelling dream or an archetypal myth. A symbol in poetry differs radically from a symbol in mathematics or one of the kindred sciences. In these it is a definite sign for something definite. In poetry it is also a sign, but, because of its multiple meanings and the feelings associated with them, points to something that cannot be precisely defined. It may be regarded as a metaphor with a rich but indefinite tenor. Yeats acknowledged his "main symbols" to be "Sun and Moon (in all phases), Tower, Mask, Tree . . ."; he also said of his lyric "The Cap and Bells": "The poem has always meant a great deal to me, though, as is the way with symbolic poems, it has not always meant quite the same thing". SYMBOLISM is the name for work that has this indefinite yet large suggestiveness. The poets known as the SYMBOLISTS flourished in France in the late nineteenth century. A **symbolist** is any poet who uses imagery, tone color, and rhythm to express indirectly the subtler play of his sensibility and often to intimate a reality which is betrayed, in both senses of that word, by the sensual world. Twentieth-century poets whose work exemplifies symbolism include Eliot, Hart Crane, and Wallace Stevens. In a poem called "Infanta Marina", which is superficially a slight lyric presenting a tropical seascape at dusk and a lady waving her fan, Stevens suggests the wide physical and metaphysical associations that attach to royalty, to wings, to ocean, and to night. It concludes:

> And thus she roamed
> In the roamings of her fan,
> Partaking of the sea,
> And of the evening,
> As they flowed around
> And uttered their subsiding sound.

symbolism   See **symbol.**

symbolist   See **symbol.**

synalepha   See **elision.**

syncopation   See **metre,** page 88.

synechdoche   See **metonymy.**

synesthesia   The intimate association of an image perceived by one of the senses with an image perceived by another. Sounds and colors are often thus intimately associated. Dr. Johnson remarked on the discovery of a blind man that scarlet "represented nothing so much as the clangour of a trumpet". Baudelaire's sonnet on the correspondences between perfumes, colors, and sounds helped to encourage the use of synesthesia by the symbolists and their successors. It is one of the chief devices of Dame Edith Sitwell, who writes of "the creaking empty light" to suggest the quality of morning light after rain, which "gives one the impression of a creaking sound because it is at once hard and uncertain". More clearly Stevens uses a visual image for an auditory one:

> At the earliest ending of winter,
> In March, a scrawny cry from outside
> Seemed like a sound in his mind.

[T]

tail   See **sonnet**, page 161; **stanza**, page 169.

tail rhyme   See **stanza**, page 169.

tailed sonnet   See **sonnet**, page 161.

tanka   See **haiku**.

telescoped metaphor   See **metaphor**, page 82.

tenor   See **metaphor**, page 82.

tercet   Three lines of verse that form a group. The term is used synonymously with triplet but is often distinguished from it as applying to three lines that do not have the same rhyme, as in the halves of the sestet in the Italian sonnet, or to the terza rima stanza. The following tercets are, respectively, from a lyric by Frost, a sonnet by Keats, and a poem in terza rima by MacLeish.

> I never happened to contrast
> The two in the celestial cast
> Whose prominence has been so vast.

> The poetry of earth is ceasing never:
> On a lone winter evening, when the frost
> Has wrought a silence, from the stove there shrills

The Cricket's song, in warmth increasing ever,
And seems to one, in drowsiness half lost,
The Grasshopper's among some grassy hills.

Graves in the wild earth: in the Godless sand:
None know the place of their bones: as for mine
Strangers will dig my grave in a stony land . . .

terza rima   A series of tercets with interlinking rhymes which give a strong effect of continuity. The rhyme scheme is *a b a, b c b, c d c,* and so on. The most famous example of the form is Dante's *La Divina Commedia.* English poets, unlike the Italian, often employ masculine rhymes, as in this example from Byron:

That destiny austere, and yet serene,
Were prouder than more dazzling fame unbless'd,
The Alp's snow summit nearer heaven is seen
Than the volcano's fierce eruptive crest,
Whose splendour from the black abyss is flung,
While the scorch'd mountain, from whose burning breast
A temporary torturing flame is wrung,
Shines for a night of terror, then repels
Its fire back to the hell from whence it sprung,
The hell which in its entrails ever dwells.

When twentieth-century poets adopt terza rima they are apt to introduce one or another variation. Thus MacLeish employed the scheme for his *Conquistador,* but used a free anapestic rhythm and avoided exact rhymes, as this fragment shows:

I here in the turn of day in the feel of
Darkness to come now: moving my chair with the change:
Thinking too much these times how the doves would wheel at

Evening over my youth and the air's strangeness:

Thinking too much of my old town of Medina
And the Spanish dust and the smell of the true rain:

I: poor: blind in the sun: I have seen
With these eyes those battles: I saw Montezuma:
I saw the armies of Mexico marching the leaning

Wind in their garments; the painted faces: the plumes
Blown on the light air: I saw that city:
I walked at night on those stones: in the shadowy rooms . . .

Auden uses terza rima with exact rhymes in *The Sea and the Mirror*, but the speech rhythm is made prominent by the use of syllabic verse:

> As all the pigs have turned back into men
> And the sky is auspicious and the sea
> Calm as a clock, we can all go home again.
>
> Yes, it undoubtedly looks as if we
> Could take life as easily now as tales
> Write ever-after: not only are the
>
> Two heads silhouetted against the sails
> —And kissing, of course—well-built, but the lean
> Fool is quite a person, the fingernails
>
> Of the dear old butler for once quite clean, . . .

In "Little Gidding" Eliot varies the form by using unrhymed lines that exhibit the terza rima arrangement in that of the feminine and masculine endings:

> 'From wrong to wrong the exasperated spirit
>   Proceeds, unless restored by that refining fire
>   Where you must move in measure, like a dancer'.
> The day was breaking. In the disfigured street

> He left me, with a kind of valediction,
> And faded on the blowing of the horn.

tetrameter   A four-foot line. See also **measure; metre,** page 88.

texture   Those details that, while requiring formal organization, may be considered apart from the STRUCTURE of a poem.
They contribute largely to its technical interest, as also to its
tone and the feeling conveyed. Such details include the modi-
fications of the metrical pattern, the associations that attach to
the words, the aural values of the syllables. For John Crowe
Ransom and his followers the texture of a poem is that which
remains over and above what can be contained in a paraphrase
of its argument.

The aural values create the specifically **verbal texture** of
poetry, what is sometimes called, borrowing the musician's vocabulary, **tone color.** Lanier declared that verse has in the alphabet "an elaborate notation of tone-colors". They are, of course,
produced by a single instrument, the human voice. Yet, as in
music tone color or TIMBRE distinguishes different instruments,
such as horn, flute, viol, and also evokes the particular emotions
associated with each, so, too, the tone color of a poem gives it a
particular aural and emotional character. The verbal texture as
well as the prose sense of "Then whets, and combs its silver
wings" is obviously different from that of "What Worlds, or
what vast Regions hold", although the lines are in the same
metre, approximate the same phrasing, and contain some of the
same sounds. The distribution as well as the character of the
vowels and consonants helps to create the tone color, as do the
diverse feelings generally associated with the short vowels in the
first quotation, from Marvell's "The Garden", and the long
vowels in the second, from Milton's "Il Penseroso". A comparison of the many details of the two poems would be necessary

to illustrate fully the difference in their textures, of which tone
color is only one feature. In *The Prelude* Wordsworth speaks of
the time when first his mind

> With conscious pleasure opened to the charm
> Of words in tuneful order, found them sweet
> For their own *sakes*, a passion and a power.

It is something of the same sort that Wallace Stevens says in a
different fashion in "The Man on the Dump", which explores
the interchange between reality and imagination that is essential
to poetry. He pictures himself sitting "among the mattresses of
the dead" and the other rubbish on the dump, which represents
harsh reality, and murmuring *"aptest eve"* . The lips barely open
in pronouncing these words, the mere sound of which suggests a
delicacy and control foreign to the dump. And then Stevens
imagines himself pulling the day to pieces and crying: *"stanza
my stone"*. This phrase has a resonance that enriches its connotations and reminds one of the elder poet who found in words
used "For their own *sakes*, a passion and a power". It is largely
the quality of their verbal texture that makes the lines that
follow vibrate in the ear and remain in the memory. The authors
are, respectively, the prolific "Anon.", George Peel, Edgar Allan
Poe, and Edward Lear:

> The Harp, the Lute, the Pipe, the Flute, the Cymbal,
>   Sweet goes the treble Violin.

> Hot sunne, coole fire, temperd with sweet aire,
> Black shade, fair nurse, shadow my white haire,
> Shine sun, burne fire, breathe aire, and ease mee,
> Black shade, fair nurse, shroud me and please me,
> Shadow (my sweet nurse) keep me from burning,
> Make not my glad cause, cause of mourning.

> So blend the turrets and shadows there
> That all seem pendulous in air,
> While from a proud tower in the town
> Death looks gigantically down.

> Lonely and wild all night he goes—
> The Dong with a luminous Nose!

See also **onomatopoeia.**

thesis   The stressed syllable in a metrical foot. It is also a term for stress. To the Greeks thesis meant the stamp of the foot or downward stroke of the hand on the utterance of a stressed syllable. **Arsis** is the unstressed syllable of a metrical foot. To the Greeks it meant the lifting of the foot or the hand on the utterance of an unstressed syllable. To the Romans, on the contrary, thesis meant the lowering of the voice on an unstressed syllable and arsis meant the raising of the voice on a stressed syllable. Many English prosodists have accepted the usage in Latin verse, with resulting confusion. See also **ictus; metre,** page 88; **prosodic symbols; quantitative verse.**

threnody   See **elegy.**

timbre   See **texture.**

tone   That feature of a poem which shows the poet's attitude toward its theme, toward a speaker or a person addressed in the poem, and toward the reader. The formality or colloquialism of the vocabulary, its vagueness or precision, the simplicity or complexity of the style, the energy or languor of the rhythms, the character of the stanzaic pattern, the use or abuse of certain technical devices, all contribute to the tone. This, of course, may shift as the poem proceeds and, indeed, often does in the work of the metaphysical poets and their twentieth-century admirers.

tone color   See **texture.**

tragic irony   See **irony.**

tribrach   A foot of three syllables, all short or unstressed. See also **metre,** page 88.

trimeter   A three-foot line. See also **measure;** page 82.

triolet   See **rondeau.**

triple rhyme   See **rhyme,** page 131.

triple rhythm   See **rhythm,** page 144.

triplet   See **couplet.** See also **tercet.**

trisyllabic foot   A foot of three syllables. See also **metre,** page 88; **substitution.**

trochaic   See **metre,** page 88.

trochee   A foot of two syllables, of which the first is long or stressed, the second short or unstressed. See also **metre,** page 88.

Troilus stanza   See **stanza,** page 169.

trope   See **figurative language.**

troubadour   A medieval poet who composed lyrics in Provençal and often also the music to which they were sung, traveling from one court to another in southern France, northern Italy, and in Spain. The **trouvères** were court poets who flourished in northern and central France during the twelfth and thirteenth centuries. It is to the troubadours, whose name is derived from a Provençal word meaning "to find", that we owe the French forms still in use. A few of their more elaborate inventions are available in translation, and their virtuosity remains the aim and the envy of poets practicing the craft today. One stanza from a poem by Arnaut Daniel, in a version by Pound, gives a faint

notion of the subtlety of their lyricism. Pound notes the onomatopoeia in the original, suggesting "the chatter of birds in autumn", and confesses that his rendering is no more than "a map
of the relative positions" of the echoing syllables in Arnaut's
canso or love song. The syllables that conclude these seventeen
lines recur in the same order in each of the six stanzas, and those
of the last seven lines are repeated in the coda.

> The bitter air
> Strips panoply
> From trees
> Where softer winds set leaves,
> And glad
> Beaks
> Now in brakes are coy,
> Scarce peep the wee
> Mates
> And un-mates.
> > What gaud's the work?
> > What good the glees?
> What curse
> I strive to shake!
> Me hath she cast from high,
> In fell disease
> I lie, and deathly fearing.

The **canzone**, a more general term for the words of a Provençal or Italian song, also refers specifically to songs relating to
love and in praise of beauty, and is occasionally used of poems
in English that bear some resemblance to such Provençal lyrics.
The title "Canzone" is used by Auden for an unrhymed poem
which uses the end words of the first twelve-line stanza in each
of the stanzas that follow, ingeniously varying the pattern. W. S.
Merwin gives the name "canso" to more than one of his

poems. These, too, are unrhymed, but key words, sometimes slightly varied, recur at unexpected intervals in successive stanzas most effectively.

An **alba** is a lyric that takes its name from the Provençal word for "dawn", which ends the refrain. It may be a religious poem but is more apt to have as its theme the parting of lovers at sunrise. A famous if nameless alba has for its burden: "Ah God! Ah God! that dawn should come so soon!". Alba is obviously related to the French **aubade**, which is also used in English for a lyric about dawn or for a morning serenade. Such is that by Davenant beginning:

> The lark now leaves his watery nest
> And climbing shakes his dewy wings.
> He takes this window for the east,
> And to implore your light he sings,
> Awake, awake! the morn will never rise
> Till she can dress her beauty at your eyes.

Another form of Provençal poem is the **sirvente**, a satire on individuals or on public matters such as the abuses of the Church or the folly of war. A **jongleur** was a wandering minstrel hired to sing the compositions of the troubadours and trouvères or the CHANSONS DE GESTE at the courts of medieval France and Norman England. The word troubadour has come to mean both a composer and a singer of lyrics and ballads. The **minnesingers**, wandering lyricists who flourished in Germany from the twelfth to the fourteenth century, were famous for their love songs.

trouvère   See **troubadour**.

truncated   See **catalectic**.

truncation   See **catalectic**.

tumbling verse   See **Skeltonic verse**.

[V]

variable syllable One which may be long or short, stressed or unstressed, according to the context. See also **distributed stress; prosodic symbols.**

vehicle See **metaphor**, page 82.

verbal texture See **texture**. See also **onomatopoeia.**

vers de societe See **light verse.**

vers libre See **free verse.**

verse The term may mean a line in a poem, especially one that has a formal structure, and is also used as a synonym for stanza, notably in hymnology. Verse "being in it selfe sweete and orderly, and beeing best for memory, the onely handle of knowledge, it must be in jest that any man can speake against it", wrote Sidney, who identified it with poetry. For the distinction between the two, see **poetry.**

verse paragraph Any grouping of lines in a poem that form a rhetorical unit similar to that of a prose paragraph. The lines need not be formally arranged in a stanza or strophe; the fact that they deal with a particular point of discourse or express the attitude of one of two or more speakers will make such a unit apparent. Thus in Arnold's narrative poem "Sohrab and Rustum" one finds these verse paragraphs:

So, on the bloody sand, Sohrab lay dead.
And the great Rustum drew his horseman's cloak
Down o'er his face, and sate by his dead son.
As those black granite pillars, once high-rear'd
By Jemshid in Persepolis, to bear
His house, now, mid their broken flights of steps,
Lie prone, enormous, down the mountain side—
So, in the sand lay Rustum by his son.

And night came down over the solemn waste,
And the two gazing hosts, and that sole pair,
And darken'd all; and a cold fog, with night,
Crept from the Oxus. Soon a hum arose,
As of a great assembly loosed, and fires
Began to twinkle through the fog: for now
Both armies moved to camp, and took their meal:
The Persians took it on the open sands
Southward; the Tartars by the river marge:
And Rustum and his son were left alone.

But the majestic River floated on,
Out of the mist and hum of that low land,
Into the frosty starlight . . .

versification   Literally, the making of verse, the term is often
used of the technical aspect of verse as it appears in practice and
as distinct from theory. See also **prosody; scansion.**

villanelle   One of the most adaptable of the FRENCH FORMS,
it consists of nineteen lines on two rhymes in six stanzas, the first
and third lines of the opening tercet recurring alternately at the
end of the other tercets, and both repeated at the close of the
concluding quatrain. With the first line as A and the third, which
rhymes with it, as A', the scheme is A b A', a b A, a b A',
a b A, a b A', a b A A'. Originally associated with pastoral verse,
the villanelle has been turned to a variety of uses by nineteenth-

and twentieth-century poets. Dylan Thomas's "Do Not Go
Gentle Into That Good Night" is a famous example. The following instance is entitled "Design":

> These part us, if at heart we are embraced,
> Their savage silence admits no reply:
> Mountains of miles, the waters, and the waste.
>
> As hungry fasts are haunted by the taste
> Of festivals gone by, the days go by.
> These part us, if at heart we are embraced.
>
> We have admired together vases chased
> With peak and cataract; now stretched eyes deny
> Mountains of miles, the waters, and the waste.
>
> Familiar streets, intimate rooms, erased
> By them, revive, but soon our minds let die.
> These part us. (If at heart we are embraced?)
>
> Fresh pleasures glow, old troubles are outfaced
> By stranger troubles, all nothing, against those high
> Mountains of miles, the waters, and the waste.
>
> The punishment for lovers who have disgraced
> Love, so divided, we begin to try.
> These part us, if at heart we are embraced:
> Mountains of miles, the waters, *and the waste.*

virelay   One of the FRENCH FORMS seldom used in English, it
is composed of stanzas of long lines rhyming with each other and
short lines rhyming with each other, the short lines of each
stanza furnishing the rhyme for the long lines of the next, except
for the last stanza, in which the short lines take their rhyme
from the short lines of the first, so that every rhyme occurs in two
stanzas. The poem is of indefinite length, but the pattern may

be exhibited in a structure of four quatrains, the first and third lines being long, the second and fourth short: $abab$, $bcbc$, $cdcd$, $dada$.

virgule   A slanting stroke (/) commonly used to indicate division of a line into feet.

vocable   An individual sound, or a word considered with respect to the sounds or the letters of which it is composed, without regard to its meaning.

vocalic assonance   See **rhyme**, page 131.

vowel rhyme   See **rhyme**, page 131.

[W]

weak ending   One that concludes a line of verse in which the last word receives metrical stress but is unaccented in normal speech and is closely connected with the first word in the line following, as the auxiliary "have" in the second line below is connected with its past participle in the third:

> Say, that I wish he never find more cause
> To change a Master. Oh my fortunes have
> Corrupted honest men.

SHAKESPEARE

weight   That quality which duration and stress combine to give to a syllable in a line of verse. It is evident in this line of Tennyson's:

> God-gifted organ-voice of England . . .

in which five of the nine syllables are both long and stressed.

Welsh forms   These stanzas use the syllabic line, but, unlike English syllabic verse, are governed by rules concerning the relation between accent and cesura, and employ rhyme schemes subtler and richer than those with which we are familiar. **Cynghanedd** (pronounced kunhánneth), mentioned under rhyme, means harmony, and is the name of certain specific patterns of rhyme, alliteration, assonance, and consonance, within the line. **Englyn** is the name given to certain tercets or quatrains, each having a distinctive syllabic form and rhyme scheme. The simplest is the **soldiers' englyn,** a rhymed tercet in which each line has seven syllables. Among other devices, Welsh verse is apt to include light rhyme and cross-rhyme. This should not be confused with CROSSED RHYME, and indeed is a more delicate echo. **Cross-rhyme** occurs when the syllable at the end of the line rhymes with a syllable in the middle of the line following or preceding it. In *Green Armor on Green Ground* Rolfe Humphries presents English poems composed in the twenty-four official Welsh metres and indicates the requirements of each. His englyn, "For a Wordfarer", is patterned on quatrains made of two seven-syllable lines, a ten-syllable line and a six-syllable line, the first, second, and fourth lines rhyming, the third line cross-rhyming with the fourth. The pattern is illustrated in this stanza:

> Sing them low, or say them soft.
> Such a little while is left
> To counterpoint the soundless drift of Time,
> Let rhyming fall and lift.

wit   The faculty that makes for metaphor by the perception of likeness in unlike things. To Dryden it was synonymous with imagination, a term that was to have a far narrower meaning in the eighteenth century, with its emphasis on reason and common sense, than it has acquired since. Pope claimed that

> True Wit is Nature to advantage dress'd,
> What oft was thought, but ne'er so well express'd . . .

Tentatively, but illuminatingly, Eliot defined the wit of certain seventeenth-century poets as "a tough reasonableness beneath the slight lyric grace". As he pointed out, it is present in the work of some twentieth-century poets. Wit is now admired as a sign of the poet's power to relate incongruities and so give a fresh understanding of complexities that neither Dryden nor Pope took into account.

word accent   See **accent.**

wrenched accent   The result of the triumph of metrical stress over word accent when the two conflict. Puttenham declared that "there can not be a fowler fault in a maker than to falsifie his accent to serve his cadence, or by untrue orthographie to wrench his words to helpe his rime". Wrenched accent is found in the work of accomplished poets when they are imitating the style of popular balladry, as Rossetti does here:

> "And many's the good gift, Lord Sands,
>   You've promised oft to me;
> But the gift of yours I keep to-day
>   Is the babe in my body."

LIST OF POETS CITED

F
B
B
Br
Br
R

List of Poets Cited